To

Carmen Westberg

Dear Jeff

A Mother's Reflections
and Responses Throughout
a Family Tragedy

Carmen Westberg

RIVER GROVE
BOOKS

Some names and identifying characteristics of persons referenced in this book have been changed to protect their privacy.

Published by River Grove Books
Austin, TX
www.rivergrovebooks.com

Distributed by River Grove Books

Design and composition by Greenleaf Book Group
Cover design by Greenleaf Book Group

All photos graciously provided by Carmen Westberg.

Scriptures and additional materials quoted are from the Good News Bible ©1994 published by the Bible Societies/HarperCollins Publishers Ltd UK, Good News Bible © American Bible Society 1966, 1971, 1976, 1992. Used with permission.

Publisher's Cataloging-in-Publication data is available.

Print ISBN: 978-1-63299-221-5

eBook ISBN: 978-1-63299-222-2

First Edition

To Jeff.

"Don't be afraid; I can't put myself in the place of God.
You plotted evil against me, but God turned it into
good, in order to preserve the lives of many people who
are alive today because of what happened."

Genesis 50:19–20, *Good News Bible*

Contents

Acknowledgments

There are many people who have encouraged me or provided practical help while I wrote this memoir—too many to mention all of them individually. If you know me, you probably should be thanked, because I might have gotten just a tiny little bit over-focused on what I was doing, especially over the past year. During this project, I know my conversations were pretty well centered on my writing, and I appreciate your interest and patience with me as I worked on this book.

I also want to thank Diana Ceres, my editor. Diana provided great direction as I was writing and shared helpful information about the process of writing a memoir. Without her, this book would not exist. Early in the process, she suggested that I read some memoirs to get more familiar with the genre. I then started reading them like I was gobbling down jellybeans. And to this day, I can't stop reading them.

There are several authors who, through their books, have helped guide me through the writing process. I specifically want to mention Mary Karr, who wrote *The Liars' Club* and *The Art of Memoir*; Anne Lamott, author of *Bird by Bird*; and Elizabeth Gilbert, author of *Eat, Pray, Love*. In addition to providing examples of good writing, they each made me laugh. And throughout this process, I really needed a good laugh now and again.

I want to thank Bill Mallory, who first encouraged me to write Jeff's story, and even promised that if I wrote a book, his wife, Tess Mallory, who is a published author, would give me some direction about how to navigate the world of publishing. Eight years later I contacted her, and she was very kind and helpful to me. She read my first draft, spoke kind words of encouragement, and suggested that I find an editor to help make my manuscript market ready. I am grateful to Tess for her careful review of my initial work and for introducing me to Diana.

And most importantly, I want to extend my deepest thanks to my family, who have been nothing but supportive while I disappeared into the world of writing. My husband, Larry, encouraged me daily, even though I suspect living with someone who is creating a book is not always that pleasant. Let's just say I was often unavailable, despite being physically in the same house. I also appreciate how Larry; our daughters, Amy and Pam; and our granddaughter Taylor all pitched in to help clarify certain memories for me. I also want to thank my brother, Bill, and my sisters, Linda, Janet, and Laureen, for all of the long conversations we had about past events. Thank you all for your support and patience. This story is just as much yours as it is mine.

Introduction

When I announced that I had started a rewrite of a book about my son, my family and friends looked at me with concern, certain that I had finally tipped over the edge into insanity. You see, I had spent two very emotional years writing our story after my son, Jeff, died. I had never written a book. I had only published two small pieces of work. One was a magazine article about our experience buying horses for our girls. The other was an article about the benefits of owning a hot tub, published in the "Home" insert of a local newspaper. So, taking on a book was a major project for me, and it goes without saying that the subject was painful. But I had a compulsion to make some sense out of Jeff's life—and a need to keep him alive in some form.

Books have been my daily companions since I first learned how to read. I knew a book would keep him alive for me, because I wear out my favorite ones by revisiting them like old friends. I frequently wander over to the Bennetts' estate, where

I enjoy the company of Lizzie and Jane and their bizarre sisters and parents. Major Pettigrew and his world draw me back for visits. I occasionally go down South to touch base with Scout, Jem, and Atticus. And sometimes, I go way back to the companions of my childhood to see what Heidi and her grandfather, the "Alm-Uncle," are up to, or maybe pay a visit to Jo Marsh; her sisters, Meg, Amy, and Beth; and their beloved Marmie, everyone's favorite mother.

So, in 2008, after I wrote Jeff's obituary, endured his funeral, and got through the immediate days and weeks after his passing, I sat down and started a book to record my memories of him. Considering that he was only with us for 14 years before his injury, I was unsure if I could offer enough content. After a lot of pacing while I stirred my brain to find a path forward, the story finally morphed into a memoir, with Jeff at the center. Often, reflecting on and reliving this difficult time proved too painful for me to continue; when that happened, I backed away for a few months before starting again. Two years later, I got to the end of Jeff's story.

And there it sat for eight years. During that time, I shared it with some family and friends. They all declared that it was very good or that they somehow hadn't finished it, but had enjoyed the part they did read. These were encouraging words, but I had to consider the source. These were people who were very close to me and who would have to sit across from me at the Thanksgiving table. I knew that I needed an objective, professional opinion. But simultaneously, I was wondering why I was even putting it out there, risking criticism, however gently it might be delivered.

I wasn't a hardened, experienced writer who had laid out her inner self before strangers many times before. I was unsure, cautious, and averse to risk. But throughout these years, I frequently had this nagging thought about getting my story out there for people to read. Maybe it could help others who might be going through a difficult time themselves. I know when I was going through this with Jeff, I had longed for something that might help me cope.

Finally, I gathered up my courage and showed my book to two professional writers. They both encouraged me to consider publishing. One of them, Tess Mallory, gave me several alternatives in going forward, but the first step had to be an editor. Tess put me in touch with an editor who specialized in memoir writing. I had mixed emotions when I emailed my book to the editor.

This editor, Diana Ceres, read my book and wrote me back, making reference to the "draft" of my manuscript and recommending a developmental edit to expand the content and go deeper into the story. This was not what I had wanted to hear! I wanted my relatives and friends back, telling me how wonderfully I had captured Jeff's story. I chewed on my bottom lip for a moment as I thought about the fact that I had already exhausted all of my ideas. I was empty, with no clue about how to approach a rewrite. The notion of revising what I thought was a completed work appalled me. I dreaded reliving that terrible time in my life for the long months of a rewrite that I suspected would need to occur.

However, in spite of my concerns, we set a time for a phone conversation, during which I told my editor that I considered my book a completed work. She then gently suggested that if I was feeling my work was in a more completed state, I could go to Kinko's and make some copies and distribute them to family and friends, because it was not yet market ready.

I then cracked open my mind a bit and listened to what she

had to say. Diana had some ideas as to how I might approach this work, and I became quite interested. As we discussed the possibilities, suddenly a rewrite went from appalling to exciting. I decided to use her suggestion of writing letters to Jeff as a vehicle to tell this story.

Jeff had suffered a severe, closed-head injury and had been in a deep coma for several weeks. During that time, I couldn't reach him and had desperately wanted to find a way to communicate with him. I told Diana about this impossible obsession I had experienced, and we decided an epistolary memoir was indeed the way to go. In writing the letters in this book, I was finally able to tell Jeff everything I had wanted to communicate during his coma, through his rehabilitation, and through the remaining years of his life.

While the events that unfold in this book are true, some of the names and places have been altered to protect the privacy of certain individuals and institutions. I hope our story can help people who are facing a tragedy like ours. Maybe it will offer some perspective. It was a scary, lonely, intense, frustrating, and exhausting time, but our family came out the other side more or less okay. While we were searching for answers, I often wanted to find a voice of experience, someone who could relate to what our family was enduring. And so I offer you our story.

Carmen Westberg,
Boise, ID, August 21, 2018

Letter 1

Dear Jeff,

We had a good start to our day, you and I. You were happy to be released from the tedium of school for summer break—which you had been anticipating since the spring, when the sun began shining so invitingly through the windows. Unfortunately, you never really liked school. I think you were born in the wrong century. I can see you as a cowboy mounted on a powerful, dancing horse, chasing the cattle north through the desert to a summer range. Or maybe you could have been a train engineer, traversing the country from the East out to the newly settled West. You would also have made a good soldier, manning a frontier fort, with forays out to battle warriors who threatened the settlers.

But today you were off to your first job—a summer job, a much tamer job—for which we had high hopes. The move from town to the country helped a lot. Of course that's because in the country, you were allowed to roam free and hang out with a pack of like-minded boys, riding your dirt bikes for hours on the trails, making unceasing noise like a stirred-up hive of angry bees. With the move to the country, you had escaped from the scrutiny of the many mothers in our subdivision who wanted quiet, well-mannered boys who would never consider taking someone's watermelon from the cooling shade of a summer lawn. What a fuss you caused that day!

I sent you off with a smile and a hug as you hopped onto your dirt bike, full of the energy of a 14-year-old boy on a new adventure. Your grandma took a picture of you just before you roared down the driveway. This was the last day of her week's visit; she was heading back home that morning.

We had a fine time doing our usual things, my mom and I. We spent a few days at the city's magnificent rose garden. You know us. We can spend hours wandering hither and yon with our notebooks, writing down details about different roses we might want to buy for our own gardens. As though either one of us needed one more rose to baby along! It's in the blood, though. In our family we are all gardeners of one stripe or another. After our rambles in the rose garden, we would find a special coffee shop and settle down for a long, cozy talk about how the rest of the family was doing. Just your typical mother-daughter time.

After waving goodbye to you, I headed to the garden and started working. Your grandma taught me how to garden. Her theory for planning a pleasing garden started out by defining the borders of her property with well-designed spaces, a mixture of perennials and annuals, trees and shrubs. And now I was trying to make memories for my kids, for you and your sisters, but somehow I didn't quite appreciate that she was planning out a typical city lot with manageable borders, and I was tackling six acres of sagebrush and native grasses.

And so I was working on defining our borders, going back into my childhood for memories to re-create. Even back then, when I was just a typical kid running around on my bike and playing games with the neighborhood kids, I looked forward to the snowbells that peeked through the snow, announcing the early spring. These early harbingers of spring were shortly followed by hyacinths and daffodils. Later came the irises and lilacs, just in time to take to the cemetery and decorate the family graves on Memorial Day. Summer brought the fragrance of roses, which occupied their own special garden in our yard, snaking around a rectangle of land that bordered the driveway. Whereas fall was decorated by the many leaves showing their colors before dropping on the ground, seemingly for our pleasure. We kids raked the leaves and then scattered them everywhere as we took turns jumping into the piles.

With these memories to draw from, I was working on landscaping half an acre plus, out of the six we live on, making it my personal mission to reduce the amount of lawn and increase the amount of garden on our property. The two perennial beds that I carved out of the yard and pasture require pretty intensive work each spring and fall. Against all reason, I also planted over 100 rose bushes that need my attention all summer—what with pruning, deadheading, spraying, and general coddling.

When you left this morning for your new job, we were having a deck installed off the back of our house. The contractor was busy hammering away as I fought a continuing battle with the pasture grass, always intruding into the flowerbeds. I remember you and your good buddy, Eric, came home for lunch, so I took a break from my gardening to fix you something. You said you liked your new job laying out irrigation pipes for the farmer. I was happy to hear that. Eric had mentioned he was also enjoying the work. The two of you had quite an appetite, and I was proud of the both of you for taking such pride in your work.

After lunch, I walked outside to say goodbye. I put my hand on your cheek and commented on what a handsome young man you were turning out to be. I waved as you drove off on your dirt bike to go back to work. If I had known how this day would turn out, I would have dragged you off that motorcycle and hauled you into the house, guarding the door with a shotgun, if necessary. But I didn't know, so after you boys rode off, I picked up the hoe and resumed my battle with the invading grasses. That is, until the phone rang.

I remember I was bending over, throwing the detested pasture grasses onto a pile, while enjoying the sounds of the contractor pounding nails into the boards of our deck. I wanted to ignore the phone. I was appropriately grubby and considered just staying where I was, but I've never been able to let a ringing phone simply exhaust itself, so I dropped the hoe and ran into the house, trying to catch my breath as I answered it.

I picked up to find a woman on the other end, the daughter of the farmer that you and Eric were working for. She told me that you'd been injured. Fear gripped me as I asked how badly you were hurt. The silence on the other end gave me the answer I feared. All I could do was hope that she was wrong. Maybe it really wasn't serious. Maybe she was just a reactionary person. But she didn't sound unreliable. She sounded reasonable and sad.

I needed to get to you, Jeff, to see for myself. I could feel the panic rising, and I couldn't seem to catch hold of my thoughts. I asked her to tell me exactly where you were. She tried to describe where the field was in relation to the road, and I tried to unscramble my thoughts and draw a mental map. I've never been good with directions, and now my mind was dancing around, unable to grab hold of and retain her words.

My thoughts then raced to your dad. I needed to get off the phone and call him. Panic started to take hold, and I didn't know which way to turn or how to proceed. Could I take the time to call the office and explain to the secretary that I really did need to speak to Larry *now*? Of course, she would immediately transfer the call, but I also had to reach you. That was the important thing. But I had to call Larry, too. He would know what to do.

I took a deep breath and made the call. We didn't speak for very long. After all, there was little to say. I didn't know much about your situation yet. I told your dad that you had been in an accident and that it might be serious. I told him where I thought you were and that I was leaving immediately. Larry always processes information calmly and rationally, and I could feel his voice trying to calm me. But I wasn't calm, and I needed to get to you. That was all I could think about, so I told your dad I would call him as soon as I had more information.

I must have looked half-crazed as I ran onto the deck, because the contractor quit focusing on his work and stood as though to block me while asking what was wrong. I had my keys clutched in my hand, still unsure of how to find you in the middle of a field just off the road, and I was probably babbling in response to his question. I turned to get by him, but he stepped forward and firmly took charge. He said he would do the driving and steered me toward his car. I don't really remember the drive. It was one of the most intense moments of my life, where I should remember every single thing, and here I am with all these blank spots in my memory.

I do know the field was about a mile from our house, right by the highway. As we drove up, I could see the truck and the irrigation pipe trailer. The contractor pulled up close to all the activity. I got out of the car and thanked him, and he drove back to the house, so he could keep working on the deck.

I looked ahead and noticed there were some men kneeling by the pipe trailer. I noticed you were lying in the dirt and some firemen were working on you. I learned later that they were trained as EMTs, but I didn't know that then. All I could see was that there were men touching you who, for all I knew, had no medical training or idea of how to treat you.

I walked over to where you were, but the men tried to prevent me from coming near you. I begged them to let me stay, saying that I had to be close by. I promised that I wouldn't interfere. "Just please don't make me leave," I cried. One of the men studied me for a moment and then nodded. I let out a quiet breath and knelt down in the dirt close enough to you, but far enough away to avoid causing the firemen any concern.

You were unconscious. You lay totally still. I couldn't see exactly what they were doing to you, because there were men on each side of you blocking my view. I was becoming very agitated that the ambulance was still not there. What could be taking them so long? These were local men—firemen and farmers—whom I might run into at the grocery store. Could they possibly know what they were doing?

I wonder why it is that we like our "experts" to be among those unknown to us. Why is it that we, or maybe just I, prefer the anonymity of a man in a white coat in a sterile office to serve as my professional, instead of the man standing next to me in line at the annual pheasant hunt breakfast? I was uneasy, unable to imagine that you were being properly taken care of in this medical emergency. At one point I cried, "Do you even know what you are doing?" They eyed me closely before assuring me that they did. So, I nodded and sat back down again.

Suddenly, pain started shooting throughout my abdomen— the kind of pain that causes you to look for immediate relief in a bathroom. I stood up and looked in every direction for the sign of a bathroom, or a place with some privacy where I could go. I noticed a woman nearby and wondered if she was the one who had called me about the accident. I walked quickly over to her and discovered that she was. She offered to drive me to her home, less than a mile away, but I wouldn't leave. I couldn't leave. The ambulance might have come.

Instead, she walked me to an area with some tall grass, where I could have some privacy; but somehow, tall grass by a ditch next to the highway didn't seem to provide adequate cover to meet my needs. And so, as the pain continued, I walked away. The woman said she thought I was having this problem because of shock. That could have been the case, but I really didn't want to deal with it anymore. Not then! I cautiously and slowly walked toward you, cradling my belly as if to hold any further pain at bay. I returned to your side and continued scanning the roads for the sight of an ambulance.

The wait for help seemed interminable. All the while, you remained unresponsive. And through all this, there were no tears. Why wasn't I crying? Why hadn't I fallen down into a puddle of helplessness in the face of this awful situation? I don't know, but it didn't even seem to be an option at the time.

Eric was also at the accident site, but I don't remember where he was while we waited for the ambulance. Maybe he was beside me when I decided that I needed to find your shoes. I remember noticing they were not on your feet. What a ridiculous thing to focus on, shoes, but I was sure you would want me to get them. Someone, maybe Eric, told me that they were with the farmer, who was sitting in his pickup truck a hundred yards or so away.

The farmer had not approached me, which seemed odd. Certainly, he distanced himself from me and the men trying to help you, Jeff. I don't remember him speaking to me as I asked for your shoes. He simply nodded, got out of his truck, reached into the bed, and handed them to me without saying a word. I just looked at him for a moment, waiting for him to speak. I found that I also had nothing to say to him at this moment. This whole scene was so surreal, rather like a dream without dialogue. I was moving through space and time without tears, almost without the ability to fully realize what was happening to my life, to your life. I just walked away with the shoes dangling from my hand to wait for the ambulance. And then I heard the siren.

Everything happened very quickly after that. The firemen had attended to you until the ambulance arrived. Once the ambulance came, the EMTs loaded you into the back, but I wasn't allowed to ride with you. I had trouble accepting that the ambulance would just drive away with you, my son, and I was to be left behind standing in a field. I was so full of fear that you might not even survive the trip, and I wouldn't be beside you. But I had to accept what they were telling me, and I immediately started searching for help.

I had no car, and I felt like there was nobody there to help me. I certainly wouldn't rely upon the farmer. As I looked around I noticed a highway patrol car was at the scene. The officer had probably been there all along, and I was just too distressed to even notice. I turned and walked quickly across the field to where he was parked. He was just next to the highway, and I remember asking if he would take me to the hospital. He said he would. I asked if he would drive fast. He said he couldn't use the siren but that he would go fast. Eric was standing by me, and I asked him to come to the hospital with me. During the ride to the hospital, Eric, a 15-year-old boy, was my support—Eric and the highway patrolman.

On the way to the hospital, Eric shared how you had been hurt. He said that you two were riding the irrigation pipe trailer to the job site—that you both had been sitting right on the braces supporting the trailer, underneath the pipes. He paused and asked me if I wanted him to go on. I nodded, and he said he didn't know how you fell—but, suddenly, you were on the ground.

What he said next has haunted me from that point on. I can barely stand to think of it now. You were on the ground and being run over. By a trailer. Eric said you cried out, "Please help me!" I have tried to block this from my memory, but it won't quite go away. Eric was shouting at the driver, but he couldn't hear him over the noise of the truck. Finally, Eric got his attention and he stopped, but it was far too late at that point. The trailer had run across your legs, across your torso, and finally over your head. Eric and I were holding hands as he got out these last details. And by the time he finished describing the events of the accident, we were at the hospital.

I saw Larry as soon as we entered. I had hurriedly asked the farmer's daughter-in-law to call him just before I got into the highway patrol car. He was standing just inside the entrance with a nun. I stopped in my tracks, afraid of what she had to say. Surely you had survived the trip to the hospital. You couldn't have died already after surviving all that time in the field. I grabbed onto Larry, who assured me that you were still alive.

You might wonder why the sight of a nun would cause such a reaction. After all, this was a Catholic hospital, so I shouldn't have been surprised to find a nun or two there. In seeing the nun, however, I could only imagine she was there to tell me that the worst had happened, that she was there as God's representative to carry me through while facing this evil. If you had died, I would have accepted the comfort of a nun or a priest and relied on them to help us cope by offering prayer and comfort.

And so, in my mind, I made that leap. But my assumption was wrong. She was actually there to take us to a private room near the emergency entrance. Before we reached this room, though, we stopped near where you were. This next part I borrowed from your dad, because it fell out of my memory bank. Larry says the space was situated so that we could see through a window. He says you were lying on your back on a table, just a few feet away. You were still fully clothed, dirty and with tire marks diagonally across your body. The marks ran from your left hip and over your stomach to the right side of your face. Larry noted how physically fit, muscled, and tanned you looked.

I simply don't understand how I could have blanked this out.

Why can't I picture you on the other side of that window? I guess it must have been all the stress and adrenaline rushing through me that day. I do remember sitting on a bench next to your dad, presumably facing this window, and saying, "It looks like we might lose our boy." He answered, "It might be so." We sat there in silence, both attempting to process this day, this horrible day that was far from over.

My next memory is of you going into surgery. The attending physician, a trauma surgeon, explained that you had internal injuries that had to be dealt with immediately. He warned us that you might not survive the surgery. In addition to the internal injuries, you had a severe, closed-head injury that could take your life before the surgery was even completed.

As we were trying to process all of this, we went to the private room the hospital had provided. I assume this room—with two overstuffed chairs, and a table and lamp between them—was for the families of trauma patients, so that they could wait in relative peace. I asked for Father Peplinski, the rector of our church, a church we hadn't been regularly attending since we moved out of Boise to the country. A hospital administrator contacted him, and he came right over, even though he probably had no idea who we were. I was so concerned for your soul, Jeff.

Were we to lose you, I wanted the priest to do all that he could. I suppose I was thinking of the last rites, if I had any clear thought at all. All I knew was that we were in serious trouble, and I wanted a priest. Father Peplinski said, in his thoughtful manner, that he supposed it would be possible for a 14-year-old to have committed an act grave enough to compromise his salvation, but he doubted it. He said that for you, Jeff, with your severe head injury, the question of salvation was now settled.

This good man, this priest of my faith, however much I had faltered in its precepts in recent years, calmed my fears for you, my dear son, as you faced the possibility of an early death.

The nun that had been standing by your dad when I arrived at the hospital took us to our private room. She was our liaison while you were in surgery. I was a nervous wreck waiting for any news about you, and the nun was very thoughtful and shared our concern for you. She would go to the nurses' station every few minutes to get us updates on your condition while you were in surgery. Finally the doctor walked into the room. He told us that you were out of surgery and it had gone well, considering the extent of your injuries. Your dad and I leaned against each other, resting in relief for a few moments.

Immediately after your surgery, they wheeled you to the intensive care unit. The nurses let us into your room for a short visit. As we approached your bed, we saw that you had been placed on a ventilator. They had also inserted a tube into your stomach, so that you could be fed. You lay in the bed, hardly recognizable to us with all of the equipment attached to keep you alive and monitor your vitals. We still didn't know the extent of your head injury. We were afraid that we might lose you in the next few hours or days.

I hated leaving you, Jeff. But we were not allowed to spend much time in the intensive care room. Our visits were strictly rationed in the ICU. Soon after, the nurse ushered us to the waiting room, where we waited to speak to the neurosurgeon who would evaluate your case. We still held on to hope. After all, you had survived the surgery. We tried to remain calm as we waited for the next piece of news. But it was hard. Everything was riding on what this one doctor would tell us. In just a few hours we would learn if you would wake up again and if our family would be intact. We would learn if all our lives would be horribly changed forever. And so we waited.

Letter 2

Waiting Room,
Intensive Care Unit, St. Alphonsus

Oh, Jeff. Your dad and I had a most disturbing conversation with one of your doctors last night, and I think I am too upset to be very good company to anyone right now. I am writing this letter to you with a wall and a swinging door between us. You are still in the intensive care unit, and your dad and I are spending most of our time in the waiting room, except when we're allowed short visits with you in your room. I wish we could be by your side all the time, Jeff. I just hate all of this waiting and not being able to sit close to you while all of this is going on.

There are many other people in this waiting room who have sick or injured loved ones needing critical care. We've all been stuck here, waiting to talk to a doctor to find out the extent of the illness or injury—as well as what the treatment protocol and probable outcome will be. In short, we've been distraught and scared, huddled together, almost like a family, trying to help each other out any way we can. And given the close quarters, as the doctors come out to give their reports, we can't help but hear the good or bad news and wonder what our report will be like when it's our turn.

Thankfully, we already know how your surgery went; we spoke to your trauma surgeon. He was very kind as he explained the injuries that he repaired, and we were so relieved when you came through much better than expected—already ahead of the curve. You are a strong young man, Jeff. But yesterday, we waited almost all day to find out about your head injury and what that might entail. We were hoping for the best, but the longer we waited, the more our worries grew.

It was such a horrible day, Jeff. I think all our reserves were depleted by just meeting each crisis as it came. How quickly life can change. One minute, I'm pulling out weeds in the garden; the next, I'm sitting in a hospital, waiting to speak to a neurosurgeon about my critically injured son, lying in a bed just a few yards away. How can anyone prepare for that?

Finally, last night, after our visit with you, we met with your neurosurgeon. Well, I'm still reeling from his visit. I can't believe how disturbing the whole conversation was. Your dad and I had been waiting all day for his report, and when he finally appeared, he was brusque and didn't take any time to answer our questions. He seemed so cold and distant, the type of person who prefers not to bother with the niceties of small talk. He walked up to us in the waiting room and basically told us that you were brain-dead. We just stood there stunned as he abruptly turned and walked away. We sat back down and looked at each other blankly, trying to process what the neurosurgeon had just told us. We didn't feel like we had enough information, but no more seemed to be forthcoming. And it was late at night, after a very traumatic day; so, we finally left the hospital and drove home to get a bit of rest before returning this morning.

And here I sit in the waiting room again, trying to come to grips with our situation. Oh Jeff, I don't think the neurosurgeon expects you to wake up. But we won't give up on you, I promise. We will be here every day to sit by your side and talk to you and care for you. You have already proven to be stronger than expected. I just know you can surprise them again.

I study your face constantly when we are together, looking for the boy who was with us just a day ago. I feel you are there, but I can't find you. You are imprisoned as much as the caged starling referred to in *Mansfield Park* who cried, "I can't get out, I can't get out."

I often felt that way—like I was trapped and couldn't get out—when I was just a little girl. I felt there was a perfect little girl that God had created, and she resided deep within me. When people didn't want to play with me, or didn't want me for a friend, I would think that if they just knew that other little girl deep inside, they would like her. And even though I knew this little girl and how she felt about people and what she wanted to say and how she wanted to act, she just couldn't get out to show them.

The other me, the one who walked about day by day, often said things she shouldn't. Words came out that she didn't mean to say. This little girl, the one on the outside, acted defensively, protected herself, and hid from people. And now you are hidden from me, deep in a coma. But I promise you, Jeff, that I am going to stay by your side and help get you out—no matter how long it takes.

* * *

The last time I helped you get out was also in a hospital. It was the day you were born. Your biological father, Tom, and I had been together four years before you came into our lives. After basic training, the army sent him to Nuremberg. At that time, I was living with his parents and working to save up enough money to join him. And within a year, I was able to. His mom made me a beautiful suit for the trip. Back then, people dressed up for the occasion, especially people setting out on adventures overseas, and I felt very adult and cosmopolitan traveling to Germany in my lovely suit.

While I was smartly dressed, I can't claim to have had much sense at that time. I was simply excited to be moving to a world far from what I'd known in Idaho. It was adventurous living in a foreign country and adjusting to a new culture. The problem was that we were young and didn't have the maturity to build *any* kind of a marriage, much less a stable one. We took a stab at it, though. We even made some friends. And I found a job typing expense vouchers for the military, while Tom went off to work each day doing soldier stuff. We had fun for a while, pretending to be grown-up, married people.

One of Tom's soldier friends was dating a German girl named Brigetta. She became a good friend of mine. Her parents, Mama and Papa, often had us over for dinner. It was Mama's goal to fatten me up. She shook her head at my "emaciated" form and served me rich stews, creamy spinach dishes, and fruit cooked in pastries with cream, among other tasty offerings. These wonderful people became my extended family while we lived in Germany.

Brigetta and the young soldier she was dating eventually got married. Mama and Papa, Tom, and I were at the train station to see them off when they left Germany for the States. As Brigetta boarded the train, she turned to look one last time at her parents, her face twisted with grief as tears streamed down her cheeks. She was leaving her country and her family for an American husband and a new land. I hoped she would find happiness in her new life.

The German girls I encountered at that time were, like me, born during or just after the Second World War. They seemed uncomfortable in their very skin, as though they carried the burden of the atrocities committed by their countrymen during the war. Coming of age with the condemnation of the world falling upon their young shoulders, these women, Brigetta included, were being worn down with guilt for acts they hadn't committed. It appeared to me that many of these girls married young American soldiers simply to escape, to outrun this heritage with a change of address.

Some months later, we left Germany to fulfill Tom's obligation to the army with a six-month assignment at a base in Killeen, Texas. Any romance or excitement we found during our adventure in Germany was certainly lacking in Killeen. The Texas countryside appeared barren and dry to my northern-Idaho sensibilities. With not even a hill to break the monotony, the only interesting memory I have concerns a trailer court. Someone had managed to find a depression in the landscape and created a small trailer park. During a Texas downpour, accompanied by Texas-sized winds, all the trailers were flooded and pretty much destroyed. When Killeen dried out, I was amazed to see that new trailers had sprouted up in the very same spot. The locals assured me that this destruction-followed-by-resurrection was routine.

Our home in Killeen consisted of a kitchen and a combination bedroom/living area, which was not enough space to challenge even my housekeeping skills. Tom only had six months left with the army, after which we would be leaving Killeen. I couldn't find a job anywhere for such a short time. We only had one car, which Tom needed to get to his army job, so I was basically "confined to quarters" for those six months.

As usual, I read a lot, but that got old after a while. Basically I was bored stiff! Tom never did take to the military life, so he wasn't too happy either. We didn't know many people in Killeen, but we tried to pass the time going to movies or hanging out with the few friends we did have. Eventually, Tom completed his tenure, and with great relief, we said goodbye to Texas and the army and pointed our car north.

We arrived in the Northwest and started to build our civilian life in Moscow, Idaho. Tom found a good job as a mechanic at a local car dealership. Amazingly enough, I landed a job with a radio station in Pullman, a small town eight miles away—as a bookkeeper. Even though I was not any kind of bookkeeper and couldn't imagine why any employer had the notion that I might be, I was grateful for the job. What I lacked in practical experience, I made up for in enthusiasm. In the interest of honing my skills, the station manager arranged for his accountant to spend a few hours giving me a crash course in debits and credits. We sat down with the ledgers spread out in front of us. The accountant's lips moved, but the sounds coming out meant nothing to my addled brain.

Armed with this extensive training, I tackled the books with determination and fervor, and, in a short time, had them in a terrible state. My boss eventually took me aside and explained that he thought my talents were being wasted in bookkeeping. He talked about adding a girl's chat show I might host—though he thought my name, Carmen, was too exotic for their small-town radio audience. He gave me a new moniker, calling the show "Coffee with *Joan*." Fortunately for us all, that never came to pass. I felt I'd have been an even worse radio personality than a bookkeeper, so I left the station.

Tom and I had just enough sense between the two of us to avoid trying to start a family at that point in our marriage. When I went to the doctor for a checkup, however, I was pronounced pregnant, in spite of our precautions. Tom did not seem to like having a pregnant wife. He was still caught up in being a fun-loving, beer-drinking kind of guy and possibly considered my growing belly a huge embarrassment. His wife, if he had to have one, should've been a sexy, flirty little thing, earning him the envy of all his friends.

If the truth be told, I wasn't much of a wife either. The daily housekeeping grind did not interest me. I didn't enjoy being pregnant, either. I felt vulnerable and scared. I didn't feel supported in my marriage, and the pregnancy added to my stress. It was like something had taken over my body. All I could think about was that the baby would grow and grow, until it eventually came out, which would involve a great deal of pain. I presented a brave face to my family, though, because I didn't want them to know what a mess I had made of everything.

A few weeks before my due date, Aunt Betty gave me a baby shower. I wasn't looking forward to this shower, as I was far from a happy expectant mother. My marriage wasn't going well, I was scared of the delivery process, and I knew it was not the right time to complicate my life further with a baby. But I put on a good act. I opened the gifts and ate the cake with a smile on my face. Surrounded by my aunts, cousins, mom, and sisters, I could almost imagine making a success of motherhood and marriage.

Despite my emotional turmoil, the pregnancy went smoothly. And when it came time for you to be born, everything went very quickly, with the doctor barely arriving in time to deliver you. I was unprepared for the rush of love that misted my eyes and swelled my heart when you were wrapped in a blanket and placed in my arms. You had a peaches-and-cream complexion, light brown hair, and I knew in that moment you were the most remarkable baby ever born.

I stayed home with you, and your dad, more or less, supported the family. He had a well-paying job, but he liked to have a nice car and time out with the guys. At that time, neither one of us were good with budgeting, planning, or getting the bills paid when they were due. While I adored you, I was alone with you all day, without a car, waiting for a husband that I didn't like much anymore. To help with money, I babysat the little girl of a friend of mine. Now, I had two children depending on me, and I wasn't even doing very well at taking care of myself. I preferred sleeping the days away while you two napped, rather than facing life head on. Eventually, I regrouped, and the gray, depressed feeling began to lift.

I started to rebound, and Tom and I made one last attempt to save our marriage. We took a trip to Seaside, Oregon. It was a wonderful week, and we almost rediscovered what had attracted us to each other in the beginning of our relationship. Soon after the trip, however, we learned that we could only get along well when we had no real-life responsibilities. Once we got back home and had bills to pay, a baby to care for, meals to prepare, clothes to wash, and a car to maintain, we found ourselves in the same old miserable marriage. I couldn't see us making it work, so I finally accepted that we needed to end it.

When I shared my decision with him, Tom, probably, was as relieved as I was, but he did the gentlemanly thing and suggested that we move to California and try again. So, I took a deep breath and gave it some thought. For a moment, I could almost see myself running along the beach with my hair—miraculously long and blonde, rather than short and brown—bouncing with every step. I, too, wanted to escape our reality and do some "California Dreamin'." But, no matter what fantasies we concocted, I just couldn't believe that Tom and I had it in us to build a good life together.

As I gave it more thought, it occurred to me that, even in California, rent needed to be paid, probably by working mundane jobs. I also had you to think about. You needed a stable life, and in Idaho we had grandparents, aunts, and uncles to help provide stability and support. And that was that. I told Tom that I couldn't move to California with him and that you and I were staying in Idaho.

Tom saw the determination on my face and knew I wasn't going to budge. Soon after the divorce was final, he packed up his things and left for California. And that's how you came to me, Jeff. And why we were living in Idaho without your dad. I'm going to keep praying that you wake up, so I can tell you more of the story in person.

Before I forget, I wanted to let you know that I called your grandma and grandpa last night. As soon as I told them what happened, they asked if we wanted them to come stay with us. I was immediately relieved—that is exactly what I wanted. I need my mother and father, too, just as you need us. They will be here later today, and I'm looking forward to having them here with us to give us much-needed support as we all process these recent events.

I am leaving now, Jeff, but I will be back this evening. I know your grandma and grandpa will want to see you, too, so I will bring them by.

I love you and will see you soon.

Letter 3

Hospital Room, St. Alphonsus

Dear Jeff,

I'm sitting at your bedside, staring intently at you for any sign of movement, any flicker of your eyelids, any twitch of your toes. So far, you are unresponsive to my voice and to the doctor's thumb, pressing into your forehead, searching for a response. I sit and wonder where you are, and how I can reach you. That may be my biggest frustration and the source of my deepest sadness: I am not sure if you can hear me. No matter how long I sit here, no matter how many times I lean down and speak your name, there is no sign that you can hear me. Wherever you are, it must be a peaceful place, maybe too peaceful for you to want to come back to us.

I haven't felt peaceful for a long time, Jeff. I feel forceful.

Probably too much so. And looking back, I can almost pinpoint when that force was born. I was 17 and standing in front of the mirror that was affixed to my bedroom door. My hands were clenched into fists at my sides, and tears were running down my cheeks as I stared at that sad little girl in the mirror. I told her she had to quit crying, she had to gather herself together somehow and think. She had to leave that home and find a room somewhere to stay, and she had to find a job to pay for that room. So, I rubbed my eyes, smeared the tears from my cheeks, and began to plan. And a force grew inside of me, the force of survival, the force of determination.

At this point, I had already made a bit of a mess of my life. I was living at home, which was not unusual for a 17-year-old girl, except that I was married. In my letter to you yesterday, I started to share how I came to be with your birth father. I would have told you when you were older. I just didn't think it was right to tell you sooner.

Life at home wasn't easy for me, Jeff. It wasn't easy for my brother or my sisters, either. Your grandfather was a difficult man who set our standards for acceptable behavior in riddles. We were not given specific rules to follow. Instead, we had to *divine* what was expected. Whenever we failed to meet his mysterious standards, he pounced on us until we quaked inside or were reduced to tears.

As you know, your grandfather has blue eyes, but they could seem as black as night whenever he was angry. He would often tell us how we'd disappointed him, meting out sarcasm and anger with black-eyed scorn. When I was about your age, my situation at home started taking a toll on me. And because I didn't believe that my father loved or approved of me, I couldn't imagine anyone else would either.

Looking back on things, meeting your birth father was pretty much the beginning of a perfect storm. We met at a school dance when I was just 15. We were a couple of mixed-up kids who were attracted to each other. Tom was cute and funny—and a great dancer. He was athletic, too. I remember he could do handstands and backflips, which I found impressive.

We had a great time at the dance that night and started dating right afterward. He was from a town about eight miles away, and we went to different schools, so I didn't really know much about him. I didn't know what kind of student he was, or if he played sports, or if he liked to swim or water-ski. But most importantly, I didn't know his character, and he didn't know mine.

After Tom graduated from high school, he chose to enter the army and suggested we get married, so that I could join him after basic training. I realized that if we got married, I could finally leave home. It's an understatement to say my reasoning skills were not fully developed back then. I think I had just shut off that part of my brain. Without giving it much thought, I simply accepted his proposal and dreamed of a life away from my father.

So, I went along with Tom's plans to elope. We met early one morning and drove to a town about 45 minutes away. I had located my birth certificate the night before. I then did a very bad job of altering my birth date to prove that I was 18. As a backup plan, Tom had persuaded his mother to pretend to be my mother. It apparently worked, because the clerk at the courthouse barely glanced at my birth certificate. After the justice of the peace pronounced us husband and wife, I quit summer school (I'd been planning to graduate early) and moved in with Tom and his parents. And Tom went off to basic training in Fort Ord, California.

It wasn't all bad. Tom's parents were basically kind people who tried to make me part of their home. His mom taught me how to cook, which became something we enjoyed doing together. His dad worked in the landscaping department of the university. When he came home, we'd have an early dinner. After dinner we'd clean up the kitchen and then settle in to watch television until bedtime. Around 9:00 p.m. the yawning would begin. Then the dog would figure out it was time to go to his doghouse for the night, and he'd get up off the floor and stretch for a minute before looking at his master to question the delay. Eventually, Tom's dad would let him out and then lock all the doors. And by 10:00 p.m., everyone was in bed.

Tom's house was very different from mine. The year I left home, there were 5 kids in the house, ranging from 4 to 17 years of age. Our home was always full of activity. There was the ruckus of the older kids coming home from school, greeted by the squeals of the younger ones still at home. There was the banging of the pans that invariably accompanied the preparation of dinner. As we all gathered around the table, your Aunt Linda and Aunt Janet would often be giggling about some shared secret. Whereas, Laureen, the baby of the family, usually had some grievance about not being included in whatever the older kids were doing. "Mom, Billy and Jimmy ran away from me today," she would whine. "Billy," Mom would say wearily, "can't you play with your little sister once in a while?" "Aw, Mom, she's such a baby. Jimmy doesn't want to hang around with my little cry-baby sister." Laureen would then wail, and Linda and Janet would continue giggling. Mom would always sigh, and I would be wishing I were somewhere far away from all of the commotion. Eventually, Dad would glare around the table and order us all to be quiet.

Tom's home was much quieter than mine and suited me for the short time that he was there with me. But within a couple of weeks, he had to go to Ft. Ord for basic training. The plan Tom had worked out with his family was that I would stay with his parents while he was in basic training. Then I would find a job and save money so I could join him at his next post. I had no car, so I needed a job I could walk to every day. Eventually, I found one at a drugstore, where I stocked shelves and rose to the giddy heights of being allowed to operate the cash register. Not a very exciting job perhaps, but I was fortunate to have it, given my lack of education and experience.

Tom's parents and I had settled into a comfortable routine. Tom's older brother, however, had other plans. He came to the house one day and told me that I was a burden to his parents and that I should not be in their home. I was intimidated by him and didn't feel like I could go to his parents for support. I had no standing in that family, so there was no room to argue my case. And Tom was in basic training, so he couldn't step in. So, I did what any 17-year-old girl would do and called my mom and explained the situation. We both agreed that I should come back home. This was not the ending I had expected when I left home to begin the great adventure of marriage.

Obviously, I was too young to have gotten married. I didn't know what it was to be deeply in love and committed to one person at that age. I was simply trying to improve my situation when an opportunity surfaced. Now, I was living in a strange world where I was neither girl nor woman.

I can't say much for my behavior during those months when I was back with my parents. I was lonely and miserable. I was not mature enough, nor committed enough, to bear the separation from Tom with dignity. Consequently, I started hanging out with some of my friends from high school.

One night, I went out with a couple of girls I knew. We didn't do much. We just rode around and stopped in at a dance to see if we knew anyone. It wasn't much of an evening, but I was pretty desperate for entertainment. I remember my friends dropped me off at home around midnight. Unfortunately, my dad met me at the front door and, because I was returning home so late, he assumed that I had been up to some unsavory activity. He looked furious as he paced back and forth. His pacing was never a good sign. It always preceded a declaration that he had come to a decision based on whatever had been rattling around in his head, probably for hours. With that familiar dark glare, he said he wanted me out of the house, stating that I couldn't live there anymore. Back then, I didn't argue with my father. First of all, it was too scary. Even adults didn't fare well in the face of his anger and belittling comments.

You've probably heard of fight-or-flight syndrome. For many years, I always retreated in flight, and that is what I did that night. Without so much as a word, I turned and ran up to my room, threw myself on the bed, and began to sob deeply. I didn't know where to go or who I could turn to.

I felt so helpless, Jeff. It just seemed that nobody wanted me around. And things were quickly spinning out of control. I didn't have any money, any way to take care of myself, a job, or a place to go. And with that realization, I got to my feet and confronted myself in the mirror. With sheer force and determination, I tried to turn a sad little girl into a woman.

As it turned out, my mother had put her foot down and told my dad that I was staying put. I wasn't there for that conversation but, knowing my mother, she didn't even raise her voice. She just told him what was to be, and my father didn't question it. It didn't happen often, her taking a stand against something he had declared. Maybe that is why when she did, he backed down. The next morning, he told me that I could stay and that he would stay out of my way, if I would stay out of his. Not exactly loving words from a father, but I had to accept those terms. They would buy me some time until I could leave a few months later to meet up with Tom overseas.

What I hope for you, Jeff, is that you can reach down deep and find that force. Just like I did when I was 17. I want you to pull yourself back from wherever it is that you are. Please, Jeff. I need you here with us. Please try, okay?

I hate to leave you, but Larry will be home soon, and I need to get back and take care of your sisters and fix dinner. The doctors say they don't know how much someone in a coma can hear. I like to think that you can hear me and that my voice will help you to come back to us. But if anyone comes in here and says anything that upsets you while I'm away, don't pay any attention to them. Larry and I have found the best doctors around to take care of you. We will be with you every day to make sure of that. We love you and will be back soon to check on you.

Keep fighting, Jeff. And sleep well.

Letter 4

Hospital Room, St. Alphonsus

I hope you had a good night, Jeff. We are getting ready for company today. Mrs. Flacker is coming to visit in a bit after her family gets together for their holiday. Today is the 4th of July, but we are having a quiet holiday this year. It won't be a bit like our usual 4th of July celebrations, when we host the migration of oddly assorted vehicles containing our relatives, streaming into our subdivision, all heading for our house at the end of Sunny Lane. What a time we all have at these reunions!

Your Uncle Bill generally leads the pack, arriving late at night after a day at work. He usually pulls into our driveway around midnight, parks his pickup, and climbs out wearily. After a good stretch, he heads for his cooler for a well-deserved beer and strolls to the diving board at the end of our pool in the back-yard. He likes to sit on the diving board with his legs dangling toward the water, while he sips on his beer and contemplates this silent night before the rest of the relatives arrive with their tents, campers, and motor homes. He might look up, hoping to spot the white owl that often cruises over the pool on a quiet evening.

Can you remember this, Jeff? This has always been one of your favorite holidays, second only to Christmas. And your Uncle Bill is certainly high on the list of your favorite relatives. And it goes without saying that you are at the top of his list of favorite relatives.

This 4th of July madness in our family started long ago, when I was just a little kid. At that time, we all headed for the farm. The farm was my favorite place as a little girl, for Grandma and Grandpa were very special to me. Their house was filled with the smell of Grandma's homemade bread, and the strong coffee Grandpa always had brewing on the trash burner, a pot-bellied little stove that seemed to belong only to him.

The trash burner had a flat, smooth top with a round lid, which you could remove to burn papers—or ticks that were found on the heads of grandchildren. Its vent carried the smoke up through the ceiling. Throughout the day, Grandpa would refresh his coffee by adding water and a handful of coffee grounds to his stove-top kettle, resulting in an inky brew that only he could stomach.

When I was little, I spent several days a week at the farm. I loved the bread fresh from the oven, spread thick with butter. For entertainment, Grandma would take me out to the chicken coop, a nasty-smelling shed thick with feathers, heat, and saw-dust; the odor rose up to fill your nostrils. Grandma and I gathered eggs from under the huffy hens, who would flap their wings in futile protest. Grandma also gave me dish towels to iron, fresh from the line. The heat from the iron released the crisp smell of the outdoors with each pass.

I remember they also kept a few cows, and at milking time, Grandpa would take my hand and lead me to the barn, where I would help milk Bossy. You know the barn, Jeff. It's that old structure with the dark hall winding from the front door to where the cow shed was, off to the side. Back then, it was soggy and fragrant with cow waste and scored with hoof prints. Grandpa hadn't believed in mucking it out too often.

Grandpa would come in for a hearty farmer's dinner midday, always driving his tractor up close beside the farmhouse. I kept watch, because the accumulated dirt that settled on the tractor was the texture of the finest flour, which I found quite suitable for my mud pies. After harvesting my "flour," I would sit happily in the yard, stirring the batter and talking to my "kids" (in my imaginary mud-pie family). At night, I would cuddle up to Grandma while she crocheted. Grandpa might haul out his fiddle and fill the room with "Turkey in the Straw," his standard fare.

We always celebrated the 4th of July at the farm. For our family, it was just a five-mile trip, but other relatives came from all over the area—aunts and uncles and cousins would come swarming out of the cars, running toward the farmhouse to get a hug from Grandma and Grandpa as soon as they arrived.

And a week or so before the holiday, Uncle Joe would go down the highway to the Indian reservation, where he could buy fireworks. We didn't have safe and sensible fireworks in those days—at least our family didn't. These were the real things—fireworks that made satisfyingly loud noises during their flight upward, before exploding in fiery, beautiful, sky-filling colors!

Long before the fireworks, Grandpa would start off the

festivities by exploding dynamite out in the field. With that ear-numbing roar, we knew the 4th had officially begun! The adults gave us kids cap guns for our 4th of July presents. Later, we drew pictures in the air with our sparklers and lit firecrackers. None of this would be tolerated these days, but I don't remember any accidents. Today, kids can't even ride a bike without a helmet. But those were more casual times, when kids were allowed to roam; climb monkey bars; play red rover, baseball, and tag; and cruise around town on their bikes, with the only rule being to return by suppertime.

At some point during the day, the pack of us kids would head for the pond, where we would catch frogs. It was strictly catch and release, and the frogs were pretty savvy, so most escaped our grubby little hands. If we got tired of frog catching, we might head for the pigpen. The game there was to climb into the pen to tease the pig. The trick was to then race toward the fence and get out before the grouchy pig could catch us. Somehow, we all escaped, which is a good thing. An enraged pig is nothing to fool around with.

Grandpa grew several crops. For a quick snack, we kids liked to eat the peas when they were a bit immature, juicy and full of flavor. He also grew alfalfa, which was our favorite crop, because we liked to create an entire "village" by mashing it down. We would each have a house with several rooms, and, of course, we needed a trail from house to house. Eventually, one of the adults would wonder idly where all the kids were and glance around for movement. If Grandpa discovered our heads bobbing in the alfalfa, he would set up a roar, "You kids get out of that alfalfa!" We would all scurry out, usually round one of the outbuildings, far from Grandpa. Only when I was much older did it occur to me that he really wasn't serious about us staying out of the fields. I think he was just doing some damage control by limiting our time there.

We also liked to go to the hayloft in the barn and climb to the top level. There was a long rope attached to the rafters. We would grab the rope, jump off, and swing through the air to the bales below. Eventually, some aunt or uncle would call us to come back for dinner. To our delight, we'd find a table set up outside. The 4th of July meal always consisted of pans of fried chicken and bowls of potato salad (as well as potato chips), deviled eggs, olives, rolls—and finally, cakes, cookies, and ice cream. And if the strawberries were still yielding, we'd have bowls of sliced strawberries with whipped cream and shortcake!

Eventually, night would fall, and we'd gather on the bank next to the farmhouse while our dads and uncles set off the fireworks. We'd always be cuddled up in blankets, because the Idaho evenings can be pretty cool. It gets dark late during the summer in Idaho. Our stomachs bulging from all the good food, we'd grow sleepy after all the excitement. The little ones might fall asleep, and the adults would eventually carry them to bed in the farmhouse, or to the car for the short trip home.

Well, I guess I've made the farm and Grandma and Grandpa sound pretty darn perfect. Well, to me they were. Grandma and Grandpa didn't have a lot of money, but they were comfortable, as best I can remember. But life was much harder back when my mom and her brothers and sisters were young. Grandma and Grandpa had six kids, a big economic depression to deal with, and very little money.

Before moving into the farmhouse I visited, they had another old farmhouse where the wind would whistle through the boards of the thin walls. When it was cold outside, the bedrooms were frigid. And when it was hot, Grandpa slept on a cot outside, in his summertime long underwear. Even at the newer farmhouse, there was no indoor plumbing until I was five or so. Before that, you had to walk up a hill to the outhouse. And water was pumped from a well just outside the door and carried into the house for dish washing and weekly bathing.

Back in those early days, there was no store-bought bread, no bottled milk, half-and-half, or heavy whipping cream in the fridge. Grandma baked her own bread and Grandpa milked Bossy—which was his name for any of the milk cows. The cream for the coffee was poured off the top from the milk jug. Butter didn't come in neat cubes; something had to be done, first. I'm still not sure I understand how churning works, but I'm pretty sure it was labor intensive. And Grandma worked hard to bake and churn and cook with whatever was produced on the farm. I heard that during the Depression, back when our parents were kids, the only items on the grocery list were salt, sugar, flour, and coffee. Fruit was always picked in season and canned.

Grandma was not slim, but she wasn't greatly heavy either. She was comfortable, like a grandma should be. When little kids climbed up on her lap for a hug, it was a soothing place with no sharp bones protruding. Grandpa was lean and of medium height. He was a gentle man, but could lay down the law when needed. Back in the '30s and '40s, a father knew who was the boss of the family. With four beautiful daughters, he always made sure any suitors interested in his daughters would be able to provide for his girls. And until they could, there would be no talk of marriage. And if he didn't think they ever would amount to anything, they were not allowed to date his daughters. All six of his kids married only once, and their marriages ended with death, not divorce. In their world back then, that was the norm.

This was our 4th of July when we were kids, Jeff, and we do our best to continue the tradition now that my siblings and I are the adults. We might be a bit more conservative now when it comes to kids with firecrackers. And after your Uncle Bill set the field on fire with a stray bottle rocket, your dad has definitely reduced the fire hazard with his "no fireworks" rule. But we still have one big, fun-filled holiday each year.

Do you remember the year that Peter came down from Canada and took all you kids on a trail ride, with our horses and all the neighborhood horses we could borrow? That was quite a sight, Peter the Canadian mounted officer and his trail of little Mounties. And do you remember how Richard always makes those ribs that he parboils and then barbecues? It's a several-hour production, but worth every minute of waiting.

Remember when Bill and Debbie set up their tent in the front yard, and I forgot to turn off the Rain Bird sprinklers? They came on about four in the morning, and Bill stuck his head out of the tent flap to see what was going on and got a direct hit in the face! He left Debbie to her fate and made a run for the house. When I stumbled into the kitchen to make the coffee the next morning, I found them sleeping on the floor in sleeping bags.

The next night, I made sure the Rain Birds were turned off, and Bill and Debbie settled back into their tents again—when they had another 4:00 a.m. surprise. This time, a big wind came and collapsed their tent. Such is life in the Wild West!

Oh, here is Mrs. Flacker. I need to stop writing for now. I promise I will finish the story later.

Dear Jeff

*   *   *

Jeff, I think you can hear me! While Mrs. Flacker was here, I asked you to open your eyes, and sweat popped out on your brow! I think you were trying so hard to open your eyes that you were sweating from all the effort. Mrs. Flacker saw it, too. Tomorrow, I will talk to your doctor and the nurses, and we will try again, okay?

I have to go now, Jeff. It is getting late, and I need to get home so your sisters can have some sort of holiday today. It is a sad 4th of July this year without you. We all love you and want you to be home with us.

Rest up. I promise I will be back to check in on you tomorrow.

Letter 5

Hospital Room, St. Alphonsus

I sit at your side, Jeff, wishing I could tell you what's in my heart, the fears I have for today. I can't speak of these things to you, even if I were sure you could hear me. I doubt that you could comprehend what's at stake, what we are all facing today and what our family is hoping for. So, in an effort to communicate with you on some level, my beloved son, I am writing another letter to you.

Today, your doctor will be coming to examine you again. I've been trying to come up with a plan to get the man to stay put long enough for me to show him what I have discovered. If I am given enough time, I just know I can reach you and bring you to the surface for a bit.

Your sister Amy first came up with the idea of trying to communicate with you through hand signals. We were so excited the first day it worked! Not only were you able to hear us, you could answer questions by using your fingers to respond "yes" or "no." It takes us about half an hour to wake you and bring you up to where you can hear and respond. And then we only have you with us for a few minutes before you sink back into your coma, into whatever space is now your comfort zone.

We have been practicing the one finger for "yes" and two fingers for "no" for over a week now. From there, I decided to raise the bar a bit and see if you could do some math. And, my dear son, you could! You were able to tell me that 1 x 1 = 1 and that 1 + 1 = 2. I did some show-and-tell with the nurses, and they got pretty excited. Nobody had any idea that your brain was this active. So far, your doctor hasn't witnessed any response from you, much less any of your communication or math skills. His procedure so far is to walk into the room, push his thumb hard into your forehead to see if he gets any response, and then quickly walk out to see the next patient.

You have been here in the hospital for almost six months, and the doctor and nurses say they consider you medically stable. The hospital staff is discussing discharging you, and the options available to us are very clear. If your brain is active and functioning, you can be accepted at the Elks Hospital for rehabilitation. If you are declared brain-dead, you will be sent to a nursing home, where you will languish in a bed for the rest of your life.

That is the sad reality I cannot—and will not—even whisper, because I couldn't bear for you to hear it. Your dad and I can barely withstand that reality. We want you to be accepted at the rehabilitation hospital, where they can help you relearn to walk, talk, swallow—all the things you used to do. We don't want to consider the alternative.

I've been plotting with the nurses. I told them I was concerned that the doctor wouldn't stay around long enough for me to show them how you can respond to our questions. Well, now the nurses are working with me to make sure we have enough time to show the doctor your progress. The nurses will give me a heads-up today as to when they think the doctor will get to your room. About a half an hour before that time, I will begin the wake-up process. I will need to have you as close to conscious as possible when the doctor walks in.

The plan is for several nurses to follow your doctor into the room and then stand between your bed and the door. They will be a human barricade, and hopefully the doctor will be trapped there for a bit. If you are awake, we will have a chance to show him that you can answer questions and solve math problems. I will be right next to you asking the questions. I pray that you will be alert enough to give him a good show.

The nurses tell me the doctor will be here fairly soon, so I am going to put this pen down and see if I can bring you up to a more conscious state.

*   *   *

I am back sitting next to you, Jeff. The doctor came, the nurses quietly made their barricade, and Jeff, you did everything we practiced. He was very surprised and encouraged. According to the doctor, what you demonstrated requires a high degree of brain function. He will contact the Elks and someone should be here next week to give you the "once-over." If you can do the same hand signs for them, chances are that you will be going to the Elks! Oh, I so hope this happens, Jeff. It will give you a chance to be on the road to recovery, whatever that may mean for you.

When it all went smoothly, when the doctor acknowledged what he was seeing, I almost buckled. I grabbed your bed railing for support and bent over, hiding my head as the tears filled my eyes. I've been so strung out, so tense, and now I can let go just a bit. Thank you, thank you, thank you for staying awake and showing the doctor what you can do. I'm going to step out for a bit, Jeff. I need to take a walk and get some fresh air after all this. Plus, I'm starving. I think I'll grab a bite to eat and a cup of coffee before I head back.

* * *

We were speaking of the doctor before I left. He has been encouraging me to go back to college instead of putting all my spare time into being with you at the hospital. I suspect that is his way of saying that I am a little *too involved* in your day-to-day care. Well, I can't help it if I want to be here, making sure you are receiving the best care possible. But I am considering his advice.

You probably don't remember that I decided to resume going to college a few short months before your accident. I interrupted my education after your dad and I were married. I did enroll at Boise College for a semester or two, but then we decided it was time to complete our family. I shed many tears over leaving school and thought my dream of graduating might have been over. When you kids were all attending school, however, I decided it was finally time to focus on making that dream come true. And then the accident happened and I stopped again. I do have my concerns that this might not be the time to resume. I still have everything else on my plate. I guess I will just see how it all goes.

Oh, I also want to share some good news with you, Jeff. Your Uncle Bill is driving down from Moscow to see you tomorrow. We will get you into the wheelchair and go outside for a bit of sunshine if the day is nice. You and Bill have always had a special relationship. What with the shortage of boys in the family, Bill welcomed you with great joy. He was so upset when we all moved to Boise after Larry and I married. You were only 2 years old, and Bill would have been 12. As we loaded you into the car, Bill cried out, "The little guy doesn't even know what's going on." And he was right, of course. You were heading off on a new adventure as we started our life in Boise.

This new adventure had really started with my divorce. Your grandpa, on hearing that I was ending my marriage, happily offered to pay for the divorce. I hadn't made him so proud in a long time! Then, he offered to pay for me to go to college. He values a college education over any other achievement, and I certainly needed to find something positive to hold on to. I needed a meaningful goal in my life. But first, I had to be accepted. He took me to the university and arranged for me to take the entrance exam. I was so nervous. It had been five years since I'd even been in school, and I hadn't finished my senior year.

When going over the results with me, the admissions representative shared that I didn't do very well in the science/math portion, but I had excelled in the English part, which is why they allowed me to enroll in college. What a relief! I was sure they would tell me I wasn't college material.

College was a tough choice for me to make, Jeff. I didn't feel like I belonged with the newly graduated freshmen, and I imagined that the students my age were smarter—and probably better people. Dropping out of high school, living a pseudo-married life with Tom, and then failing at that marriage all contributed to my feelings of inadequacy. Luckily, I soon ran into one of my old high-school friends, Corey.

We gravitated toward each other in high school because neither one of us really fit into the crowd. We were probably a bit socially awkward and had our heads in the clouds of literature and art. I was consumed with reading every book ever published: I would haunt the local library, returning home with as many as I could carry. My plan was to start with the A authors and keep reading until I plowed my way through Z. Corey, meanwhile, was busy drawing everything in sight.

We talked about music, art, and literature—and how we wanted to live out our lives. She wanted to be an artist when she grew up, and I fancied that I might someday become a writer. We were very different in many ways, but we could trust each other with our dreams.

Corey was more competitive than me at that age. That was a trait I developed later. I remember a day when we were at the city recreational center, where she was playing Ping-Pong with anyone who would challenge her. I remember boys coming forward to take her on. Corey flew from side to side, striking with that paddle, slamming the ball over the net really low, so that it hit just on the edge of the table. The boys drifted away after the game, and she looked after them a bit puzzled. After all, hadn't she just demonstrated what a good player she was?

She was also more uninhibited. We would often meet at her house—it was larger than mine and less cluttered with younger siblings. One day, she put a classical record on the stereo and, as the air vibrated with sound, we twirled and leapt around the living room with our rendition of ballet. I was a bit embarrassed (and glad nobody else was watching), but she seemed to enjoy it fully.

We shared an interest in trying to beautify our young selves. To that end, we were in charge of each other's eyebrows. Hers were dark and thick and needed more aggressive grooming than mine. Tongue in cheek, she claimed the bloody gashes would need to heal before I could get after them again.

Corey never approved of Tom, and she was determined to find me a more suitable mate. With an entire college campus to choose from, she put her agile mind to the task. She'd selected a young law student named Dan for me. She decided that a law student from a wealthy family would be just about perfect for redefining my life. Unfortunately for her, neither Dan nor I were particularly interested in forming a union.

She set up a meeting for us at a college hangout. Corey accompanied me, and Dan brought along his roommate for support. It turned out that the roommate, not Dan, was the man who would redefine my life. Larry and I had known each other in high school, and despite Corey's best efforts to get Dan and I to date, I was far more interested in getting reacquainted with Larry.

Larry and I spent that entire evening catching up, and began dating soon afterward. Dating him was like entering a whole other world. He taught me how to play bridge. We went out to dinner, watched football games, and attended parties. We even took a ski trip to McCall with another couple. The Idaho mountain town was covered in white; we were in a Currier-and-Ives winter wonderland, snow piled up alongside the road, decorating the trees and frosting the roofs.

That weekend was a break from my new role as a student. And I needed a break. I'd been playing catch-up since the moment I'd gotten there, as it had been five years since I'd even stepped into a classroom. I found a tutor to help me through the college-level math course. (Math was always a challenge for me.) But as the year went on, I slowly gained confidence academically—and socially. The social gains were possibly harder-fought.

Most of Larry's friends were members of a fraternity as well as law students. Their girlfriends were garnered from sororities, and their lives appeared to be uncomplicated. I wanted to join this charmed circle, where life progressed from high school cheerleader, to sorority girl at college, to blushing bride of a promising young law student, architect, or accountant. I wanted my problems to be more along the lines of deciding whether to get married before or after graduation, to have a church or garden wedding, and to honeymoon in Hawaii or California.

During this time, Larry invited me to a cocktail party at the home of one of his professors. In those days, I had nothing resembling a proper cocktail dress, so Mom loaned me the money to find just the right thing. I bought a simple, sleeveless, lightweight black dress. Your basic cocktail dress, right? Larry picked me up, and we drove to the professor's house, which was perched on a hill by the campus.

As I clung to Larry's arm, we walked up to the door and were ushered out back to the garden, where the guests were assembled. As I looked around, I was horrified to find all the other women in sundresses. I already felt very out of place, and this just put the cap on it! I walked away by myself, when I had the chance, and stood by a fence, pretending to enjoy the view. Soon, Larry was by my side, and that was a comfort, but I still had a deep longing to fit in, to be one of those uncomplicated girls that I saw as having had, shall we say, a less dramatic life.

But our reality, Jeff, was a bit different. You spent time at the sitter's or your grandma's house while I went to school and cautiously reentered the single world. Before I connected with Larry, I had been leery of the dating scene. I didn't trust myself in choosing a boyfriend, but I quickly developed a system. If any guy that asked me out showed any traits I identified with Tom, I refused to date him. That may seem a bit harsh; I had changed for the better, and so might he have. Let's just say that I wasn't looking for a "fun" guy. I'd done that and learned the consequences. If I got involved again, it would be with a man interested in building a stable, predictable life. And I didn't have much spare time anyway. I was a newly single mother and a fledgling student, and I had a part-time job.

I did find time to date a couple of guys that didn't remind me of Tom, but I wasn't sure that they fulfilled the "stable and predictable" requirement. I met the first guy when I was out with the art and music crowd. I don't remember why he was hanging with the college kids. He wasn't a student. We talked about books mostly, a subject that could keep me going by the hour. Not long into our relationship, he invited us to go live with him on some mountaintop in Washington. He had a job watching out for forest fires, and a shack perched on the mountain was part of the deal. I declined that offer without any need for further thought.

The second guy I met seemed nice enough. I met him at a party, and I think we went to the movies. He asked me out again and showed up on my doorstep armed with a white rose—and the assumption that we were an item. I explained that I was not interested in a serious relationship at that time, and he turned away with harsh words for me and all other Idaho women.

Larry and I dated for about a year before he graduated from law school. After graduation, he went to Boise to take the bar exam. He was worried that he wouldn't pass. I was confident that he would, and he did. Not long after that, he went back to Boise to apply for a job. I was sure our romance was over. I enrolled for the coming semester, and he hadn't yet said a word about the prospect of "us." I felt so empty, imagining him contacting his old girlfriend, who I knew lived in Boise. You and I, Jeff, would be left in Moscow. It seemed I would continue going to college, and Larry would begin his new life as a lawyer in Boise.

As fate would have it, Larry was offered the job and came straight back home. He called me to share the good news and suggested he come by so we could take a drive. We drove out into the countryside, where we parked by a grove of trees overlooking the Palouse farmlands. We loved this land; both of us had grandparents who had built up substantial farms, still held by our families. We talked about how nice it would be to have a home overlooking these familiar hills someday. He then turned to me and asked me to marry him, and I wholeheartedly accepted.

Because his job was in Boise and he was leaving soon, we decided to start our lives together sooner rather than later, although that meant I had to interrupt my college semester. We both also realized that I needed time to recover from a difficult childhood and a failed marriage. But we were in love and this was our time, so we held hands and jumped!

I don't know if I ever told you this, Jeff, but Larry and I were married on your grandpa's birthday, October 19. I liked the idea of being a fall bride. Autumn has always been my favorite time of year. I love the cool, crisp snap to the air when all the deciduous trees turn even more beautiful. I enjoy the leaves, burnished red and yellow, as they show off their colors for a while before floating down to the sidewalks.

Darkness arrives by late afternoon in northern Idaho in the fall, which sets a solitary mood. When I was about 10 years old, I attended Camp Fire Girl meetings one night a week at the Methodist church about a half mile from our home. Afterward, I would walk home through the silky dark of early evening, smelling the fall air and listening to my feet moving on the pavement as I scattered the crisp fallen leaves.

When I was a kid, I was a little uneasy about walking home alone in the dark, but I also felt a strange enjoyment in moving through the lonely dark of night. Others were with their families behind lit windows; I traveled unobserved, like a ghost moving quietly along the sidewalk. With these memories in mind, I was very happy to be married in the fall, as it felt like a special season for all of us to be starting our new lives together.

When we were planning our wedding, we decided to keep it simple. For one thing, we were totally broke. Larry had put himself through law school, and I just had a small part-time job. Your grandpa was paying for the wedding, so that wasn't a strain on our extremely limited funds. But I found myself reluctant to plan a traditional wedding—with the white dress, veil, and dozens of people I barely knew witnessing a very personal event. I was probably embarrassed by my unfortunate first attempt at matrimony. I was a bit young, for one thing, to already have an ex-husband. I thought it unseemly that a 23-year-old bride had already racked up 5 years in a previous marriage. Instead, I wanted a simple Catholic wedding in my church that would be witnessed by just our families.

Larry and I were married in the Catholic Church, which signified to me permanence and a sacramental commitment. Being married in the Church was more important to me than a white dress or any other trappings. We said our vows before the priest, the small congregation, and before God. I wore a suit, and Larry wore dress slacks and a sports jacket. Your Aunt Linda was my maid of honor, and our friend Harry was the best man. We had a small wedding and a blowout reception at the Elks Club. Your grandpa finally had them take away the open bar after a couple of hours. My great uncle Matt, a very frugal man, looked quite sad as it was wheeled away. It wasn't often that free liquor came his way.

I doubt if you remember any of this, but you stayed with your grandpa and grandma for a week after the wedding. After the reception, Larry and I hopped into his '56 blue-and-white two-door V-8 Ford Fairlane and headed south to a small Idaho mountain village for our wedding night.

Whoops! Where did the time go, Jeff? Here it is pushing five o'clock and I need to head out. We had quite a big day, didn't we? I am so proud of how hard you worked to climb up out of that deep place where you are now. I will be back in the morning with your Uncle Bill. Remember how much we all love you and hang tight. It's looking like we'll be able to get you out of here soon!

Letter 6

Elks Rehabilitation Hospital

Jeff, I know you are tired after your therapies today. I will just sit here for a bit and keep you company, even though you are deep in that semiconscious state where you retreat. I just spoke to the social worker, and she went over your progress with your therapists here at the Elks. You certainly have lots of people here to help you. You have a speech therapist, a physical therapist, and an occupational therapist developing detailed plans to help you talk, swallow, sit up, regain balance, and hopefully walk again. You also have a psychologist, and I'm still trying to understand how a psychologist will develop a working plan to help someone who can't really talk and is often in a semi-coma.

Maybe the staff psychologist has his eye on me and plans on getting me into therapy. I seem to be developing some weird habits. For example, I can't seem to slow down for a minute. If

I do slow down, I think. And if I think, I feel. And if I allow myself to feel, I'm afraid I'll just collapse into a useless puddle. Rather than reflect too much, I push all my fears and sadness into some deep place inside and just keep going. It's much easier that way.

And even with all this activity, I don't seem to find much joy in my days. In fact, everything seems very gray. My doctor thinks I'm depressed and wants me to take some medication. If this is depression, it is very different from what I thought depression would be like. It isn't like I feel totally sad all the time. Mostly I just don't feel much at all. If your dad asks if I want to go out to dinner, I don't care where we go. If he asks if I want to go to a movie or take a walk, I really don't have an opinion on that either. It doesn't seem to matter much one way or the other.

Yesterday, after our visit, I went home. Soon after, the girls arrived from school and plopped down on the floor in front of the TV. Your dad wasn't home yet. Ever restless, I wandered out into the pasture, crossed the stream, and sat down on a bank. I felt so tired and drained. I just laid my head on my knees to rest a bit. Pretty soon, I was sobbing, deep sobs that completely took over, that I couldn't check. Suddenly, I felt something behind me blowing softly on my neck. I turned my head to find our horses, each with a muzzle by one of my shoulders. And they just stood there behind me while I cried, waiting patiently until I was all cried out.

Eventually, I got control of myself. I rubbed my fists over my eyes to remove most of the tears. Then I stood up and put my arms around the neck of each horse, feeling their body warmth as I pressed against these furry friends who had given me comfort. I then turned toward the house. There was dinner to prepare, homework to supervise, and even my own homework to do. Then there would be the short reprieve of sleep before starting it all over again the next day. And most important of all, we have the "Jeff Project."

I want to be involved in all that you do, Jeff. I feel a need to be by your side, encouraging you to try harder, so that you can give it just a bit more effort. I've noticed that when you hear my voice, you'll usually try again. I know this is very hard work for you. I also know that each movement, each stretching of a limb after so long a time just lying in bed, causes you a lot of pain.

You don't seem to have many reserves to draw from. I think you would rather just drift away into that place of peace where you've been for over six months now. But if you are to have any kind of a life at all, we have to break through that barrier. I don't know how far we can bring you back, but I want my boy back. I want the boy who defied gravity on the ski slopes to return. I want my boy who preferred it when the horse bucked and who drove the neighbors crazy riding his trail bike by the hour with his buddies.

I remember a day, just before your accident, when I was driving home from work and noticed a familiar figure in front of me on a motorbike. I was only a mile or so from our house, but decided that it couldn't be you. You were forbidden to ride your motorbike on a road outside of our small subdivision. But when I got a bit closer, I saw that it was indeed you, my son.

As I followed you up the hill, you were clearly having the time of your life. Your hair was dancing in the wind. Your whole body showed signs of great pleasure as you tore up that hill, at one with your bike. And I couldn't help smiling while I, your mother who had forbidden this activity that was giving you such joy, witnessed this transgression as I followed you home. Oh, Jeff, please try hard and come back to us. I never thought I'd say this, but I miss your mischievous ways!

Now, the physical therapists are simply trying to get you to stand between stabilizing bars that can bear your weight. Your once-muscular body is now slack. And you have one side that is more impaired than the other, like a stroke victim. I watched as the therapists sat you on the exercise ball, helping you balance while you bobbled around like Humpty Dumpty. I'm not even sure how much you see these days. Your left eye is bulging out a bit, and you can't seem to open the lid on your right eye. Oh my handsome boy, this is all so hard to accept.

Your occupational therapists say they will help you relearn to swallow. They tell me that it's a very complicated process. And then there are the voice lessons that you get from your speech therapist. When you do make a sound, it's in a monotone voice that you produce on the inhale. Your speech therapist says that this is damaging to the voice box.

Once you are more stable, your physical therapist will put you in the pool here at the Elks. They tell me that the pool is a great place for you to work out, because the water helps support you. You also won't get hurt if you fall, and the water is a safe force for you to push against.

Our social worker told us that once you can eat solid food and walk unassisted for a bit, we'll be able to take you home on the weekends. We're all hoping that day comes quickly. I want you sleeping in your room again, even if it's just for a night or two a week. It's so hard for me to walk away each day and leave you here, especially because you are so upset when I go. But eventually I have to leave. I have your dad and the girls to take care of, too. Your poor sisters. I feel like I'm not being the best mother to them right now.

I wish I could find more comfort in prayer, but I haven't been going to church regularly. This isn't your fault, Jeff. It's not because I'm here every day. I just haven't been practicing my religion faithfully for some time. When we moved into the country, it wasn't convenient. Then weeks, or even months, would pass without me trying to attend church. And now, I really need to find some spiritual peace. But I'm not sure God knows who I am anymore.

When I was a kid, we attended Mass every week. Our religion was reinforced in school, because all five of us kids went to Catholic grade school. Every Sunday, Mom would dress us up for church and, usually a bit frazzled from the struggle, load us all into the car for Mass. Our dad would stay home, probably sleeping in front of the radio, listening to a game or a boxing match. He wasn't Catholic and rarely went with us—just at Easter and Christmas.

When we got to church, Mom would steer us to the left side of the nave, about halfway down. She liked to sit on the end of the row, by the window, so that if she got too warm, she could get up and crack it open. Maybe she had a slight case of claustrophobia and would get dizzy—I'm not sure. If we didn't sit still and behave during Mass, Mom would reach over and give us a quick pinch. While the congregation remained ignorant of her stealthy disciplinary methods, that signature move corrected our behavior.

I don't think I ever told you this, Jeff, but when I was about 9 or 10, I was so into my religion that I even thought about becoming a nun. It was probably the influence of the nuns at

St. Mary's school. Well, some of the nuns—the ones who were nice and fun to be around. Mother David comes to mind. She was a young nun and not above joining us kids whenever we played games.

I remember one afternoon when we were playing baseball on the school grounds. She came onto the field, hitched up her long, black skirt, and tucked it into her "holy" belt. Then she grabbed the bat and joined in on the fun. I suspect she was a bit of a tomboy before taking her vows.

Some of the nuns still ramble around in my brain with no more impact than the schoolbooks, the desks, or the classrooms. They were there, but have faded more into the background. And then there are two nuns who really stand out. Both of these nuns, Mother Carmel and Mother Anthony, were old. In fact, Mother Carmel taught my mom and her sisters, and they still squirm around a bit when they remember being in her class. We all feared her a bit, too, but we didn't feel particularly picked on when we were the ones facing her wrath. She didn't pick on anyone in particular. She just kind of rotated her way around the room until a student did something meriting her attention. And it was usually a boy.

Mother Anthony was another story. She was very old. She looked to be about 110, but I doubt she was that old. I remember she drooled and frequently dabbed at her mouth with a sodden white handkerchief. She didn't seem to enjoy teaching and was prone to unpredictable fits of anger. One day, I was the unfortunate object of her rage because of a math problem.

At the time, I wasn't terribly excited about studying multiplication and division. I was more interested in English, where there were books to be read containing exciting new words I didn't quite understand yet. That day, I must have been particularly dense about some equation, because Mother Anthony hurled an arithmetic book at me. I didn't even bother to complain to my parents. In my world, these things were best endured and kept to myself. I knew that if my behavior merited getting in trouble in school, then I would be in even more trouble if my parents found out.

I still felt drawn to become a nun, in spite of these two examples. Sometimes at night, I would put on my white flannel nightgown and imagine that I had taken my holy orders. I might even hold a rosary, dangling from my fingers and clutched to my chest in a prayerful manner as I walked around my bedroom. The nuns lived in a convent across the street from our school. We often were on the grounds and in the convent itself, but we were never allowed in the back areas where the nuns had their private rooms. I very much wanted to peek into that private area, but I never did.

Their private quarters held a strange fascination for me. I wanted to see how the rooms were organized. I wondered if the beds were stark and uncomfortable-looking. I also wondered if they had any ordinary clothes hanging in their closets and if they were allowed to have hairbrushes. Certainly it was just a rumor that they shaved their heads! Were they allowed to have books on a bookshelf? That deprivation alone probably would have discouraged me!

One of my favorite things was the life-sized statue of the Blessed Virgin Mary, which was displayed proudly on the school grounds. On the first of May, all the students would march in procession from the school, past the kindergarten area where Mother Ursula kept loving watch over her "babies," to the statue of Our Lady. We would all sing, "Oh Mary, we crown thee with blossoms today; queen of the angels, queen of the May," as one chosen student placed a beautiful wreath of blossoms upon Mary's head.

But when I was around 13, I started drifting a bit from my faith. Hormones were affecting my emotions, attacking my brain, and changing my body. My focus shifted, and I became interested in boys and dancing and music. Church somehow became very boring.

By the time I was 17 or so, I became disenchanted with the orthodoxy of the Catholic Church. I thought (although that word is most likely too generous a description of the process) that old men in dresses shouldn't be dictating behavior to a bright freethinker of the 1960s like me. So, with the accumulated wisdom of a teenager, I set off to discover a more *reasonable* dogma.

This dogma, of course, would be consistent with my feelings about what was right and wrong. Instead of going to church, I would follow my conscience. And in doing so, I created a much more understanding and lenient God. In fact, I think this process simply elevated me to His level. And since I didn't educate myself with any Bible reading or theological study, I found very little to challenge my conclusions.

I didn't officially break off from the church. That would have taken a courageous and conscious act. I simply decided which parts of the Church's teachings were reasonable and which were not. This allowed me to be nominally Catholic while not irritating my extended family members by openly defecting, so to speak.

And now here I sit next to you, badly in need of some spiritual comfort and with nowhere to turn. While Father Peplinski came to St. Alphonsus, to sit with us while we waited to see if you would even survive the accident, he isn't my priest. And since I don't attend any particular church regularly, I don't even have a priest who would recognize me.

In spite of that, I pray to God all the time for your healing, and I ask God to give me the strength to deal with this trying situation. And sometimes, I feel like I am heard. Sometimes, I feel peace flooding through me, a peace I cannot explain, as I beg God for help. But it is fleeting. And maybe that is how it's supposed to be, since I have become so lax and indifferent to matters of faith.

I seem to be a bit gloomy today. Whenever I speak to you or I interact with your different therapists, I push all these feelings aside. I guess I save them for when you are sleeping and I am sitting by your bed for long periods of time. I must be saving them all for these letters.

It is time for me to leave you again, Jeff. We both need our rest so we can start again tomorrow. Goodnight, my son.

Remember that we all love you.

Letter 7

Elks Rehabilitation Hospital

Dear Jeff,

I am thinking something is in the wind at the Elks. During the last month or so, the therapists have encouraged me to become more directly involved in your therapy sessions. I don't know if this is in preparation for your discharge, or if they were simply wanting to get me up to speed before we started your weekend visits. So far, even though you have been cleared for weekend visits, there has been no sign that you will be discharged soon. It does seem, however, like your physical therapist has been trying to turn *me* into a physical therapist, too.

For example, she has been pushing me to learn some specific floor exercises, instead of just providing encouragement to you during the sessions. They have also asked me to participate in your pool exercises at the Elks. And they have been very interested in the fact that we have a pool at our home. You know I have always liked helping with your therapy, but it makes me a bit nervous to think about working with you on my own, if that is what they have in mind.

Maybe I'm just getting ahead of myself and all that preparation was simply for your weekend visits. I'm so relieved that we are finally allowed to pick you up before dinner on Fridays and keep you until late Sunday afternoon! We love having you come home with us on the weekends, now that they've given you the clearance to do so. You worked so hard to learn to swallow again, to improve your balance and walk (with help), so that it would be possible for us to take you home.

We are so proud of you, Jeff. Walking you into the house that first weekend all by ourselves felt like such a big step. And then there we were, all of us finally together in our living room, your sisters snuggled up by your side. We felt like our family was complete again. And I could finally take a deep breath and quietly let it out for the first time in a year.

Do you remember your first weekend back home? You were tired out from the anticipation of your visit. And then there was all the effort of getting into the car, and the ride from the Elks to our home, and then getting out of the car, and, finally, walking into the house. All these normal activities take a lot out of you, Jeff.

After dinner, we got you settled down for the night. I realize this was a bit early, but we wanted you to rest from your long day at the Elks and the excitement of coming home for the weekend. When we put you into your bed that first night, it was like the answer to all our prayers. What contentment, what joy we all felt. And you drifted off to sleep quickly. I remember I couldn't quit opening the door to your bedroom and looking at you sleeping there. I'm glad you didn't wake up. It might have been a bit unnerving to open your eyes and constantly see me peering into the room at you. But I could hardly believe that you were back home with us. I guess I just needed to keep checking to make sure it was really true.

Our routine now includes giving you some physical therapy during your weekend visits. You are a bit more cooperative at home, with me, than you are at the Elks with your physical therapist. That is a good thing. I don't want to have to get tough with you when we only have this short time at home together each week. And, in fairness to your therapists, they have had to push you very hard to get such good results. You have traveled a long way, young man, from when you were taken from the hospital to the Elks. At that point, you couldn't walk, roll over, talk, swallow food, sit up, or do much of anything without help. Now look at what you have accomplished!

Your dad and I have decided to remodel our house. It has become clear to us that your small bedroom won't be suitable when you come back home for good. We think you will need your own bathroom and a larger bedroom. We have been meeting with a contractor who will build us a new master bedroom and bath within the footprint of our current garage.

We will eventually have a new garage built, too. It will be separate from our house. You will take the current master suite, and we are going to have handrails installed throughout the bedroom, bathroom, and down the hallway, to help you move about safely. All this construction will be a bit of a disruption for a while, but we want to get this project completed as soon as possible, so that your area will be ready when the time comes.

I'm not sure how much help we will get from the Elks after you are no longer an inpatient. We haven't completed our research yet to find out what community resources are available to us. For a year now, we have been totally absorbed with what was happening at the hospital, and then at the Elks. We were just trying to handle the problems that each day threw at us. But we should probably start looking into some options for you.

Keep up your hard work, Jeff. We want you to make all the gains you possibly can while you are at the Elks. I will see you tomorrow. Remember, we all love you and want you back home with us.

Letter 8

Country Home, Idaho

Jeff, I am sitting in our living room, reflecting on our lives over this past year you have been back home with us. We were all so hopeful for your happiness and improvement once you completed your rehabilitation and could finally come back home where you belong. We were so happy the day the Elks told us that their work was done. I remember being called into the social worker's office to discuss your transition home. You had been under constant professional care for a year, except for short visits home on weekends, so I was excited to hear their plan. When I asked the social worker who would be in charge of your care, now that you were leaving, there was a big pause while she arranged her thoughts.

When she shared that we would now be in charge of your care, I was a bit speechless—and you know I am seldom speechless.

I just stared at your social worker, waiting for her to give me something, anything: a plan, a suggestion, a contact. But, she had nothing. Well, that's not completely true. She said they would assign a physical therapist for home visits, as needed. But arranging physical therapy was the easy part. I was more interested in how we would manage all of your medical conditions, whatever they might be. We knew your vision was terrible, that you couldn't raise one eyelid or see much with the other. Who knew what else was going on inside your body! You had been run over by a trailer loaded with irrigation pipe, for God's sake. And then there were all the psychological issues you were facing. You were once a very active kid. But now you can't walk or run like you used to. And you are just a kid still, only 16. How were we to help you through all this? At the very least, we needed an instruction manual, not a pat on the shoulder and a "good luck to you" from the hospital.

Oh, Jeff, this was all so overwhelming. I simply didn't know how we would begin to care for you by ourselves. In that moment with the social worker, it felt like someone had just punched me in the stomach. Your dad and I have no skills or training in this area, and there are apparently few resources available to help us here in our community. We eventually found a psychologist to consult with, and we arranged for some at-home care during the day, but our limitations and our lack of training and knowledge became evident very soon.

Before the accident, you were changing from a rambunctious boy into a handsome young man, and the girls at your school had been noticing. They started calling. Back in my day, girls never called boys. Instead, we were supposed to wait, ladylike, for the phone to ring. Apparently, all of that has changed. Girls were on the line, asking, "Can I talk to Jeff?" When I handed you the phone, you would look at me with puzzled brown eyes, perhaps wondering if I could make the calls stop for a year or two. Well, that time has passed, but not the way any of us could have anticipated. And now, you are not the same boy you were before the accident.

The remodel was finished before we brought you home, and we were anxious to show you your new quarters. Unfortunately, we were missing a piece of information. We didn't know you hadn't looked in a mirror in all the time you were in the hospital. Amazingly enough, you didn't look into the mirror when you were home for your weekend visits either. We always helped you into the bathroom and stayed there with you until you were finished. But when we brought you home to stay and led you into your own private bathroom, you were confronted with the big mirror over the counter. In that moment, you froze as you stared at your reflected image in the mirror.

You didn't have very good vision, but you had enough to realize how much your appearance had changed since the accident. I felt so sad and helpless as you cried, staring at the harsh reality in front of you: one bulging eye, one closed eye, and limited movement on one side of your face. I wish I had known that you hadn't seen your reflection, so that I could have prepared you better.

Instead, I stood helplessly next to you as you realized for the first time how much you had changed. My heart was heavy. I wished I could have done more to help you, to make things better. But all I could do was hold you tight. I hope that I was able to give you some comfort in that moment, Jeff. And I hope that you know that we love you all the same, no matter what that accident did to you.

* * *

It was summer when you returned home. The occupational therapists said that our swimming pool would be a good place for you to exercise. Jill, our favorite occupational therapist, came out and gave us instructions on how to work with you in the pool. Do you remember those sessions, Jeff? How your dad or I would walk backward with our arms outstretched, as you walked toward us against the force of the water? Jill said using the resistance of the water would help you build muscle mass and improve your balance and coordination.

I felt like I could take a bit of a deep breath during these sessions in the pool. You were safe in the water with us close by. And I took comfort in the fact that if you fell, you would simply hit the water, not the hard ground. I remember that after therapy, you liked to be helped onto a float so that you could just drift along, absorbing the summer heat, maybe forgetting for a short while that your life had changed so much.

Soon after these successful sessions in the pool, your dad and I became focused on finding some additional activities that you would enjoy. Jill thought you needed to get excited about something—anything that would engage you to push harder to get better. I'm not sure who came up with the idea of putting you on one of our horses. So far, you were just going along with other people's ideas for your therapy, and maybe I mentioned to Jill that you used to love riding. Maybe Jill noticed them in the pasture and saw the possibilities for therapy. Whoever first suggested it, that summer, we all decided you would take up riding.

Looking back, I think it worked in our favor that our horses were like big pets. We definitely needed a calm horse for this procedure, and Buddy was a great "therapist" in that way. For your riding lessons, we would roll your wheelchair out to where Buddy was tethered. Then Jill and I would push and haul you up into the saddle, standing on either side of Buddy to help stabilize you.

For your first session, you bobbed and weaved around a bit too much for our comfort, although you had a firm hold on the pommel. We still walked beside you, in case you started to slide off the horse. It was a calm, short ride, which we considered a success. Unfortunately, the next time you mounted Buddy, you had it in your head that you could gallop around like you used to, and you wanted us to step aside and allow you two to have some fun. However, you lacked an awareness of the dangers of riding independently. Given your inability to balance yourself, you were barely able to stay on board *with* our help. We had to be very careful, or you would be badly injured. In the end, we realized that we didn't have enough control from the ground to keep you safe, once you were in the saddle, so we decided horseback riding wasn't a good idea, and we stopped the sessions.

Still looking for a good outlet for you, we thought about how you always loved going to the fair that came to town each fall. We used to go as a family, your dad and I, you and your little sisters. Once you were older, you met up with your friends and went off with them for a time, clutching your ride tickets in your hand. I remember that you loved the bumper cars most of all. You'd put the pedal to the metal, fearlessly ramming into your friends' cars, slamming them into the padded outer walls.

When the fair came to town this fall, we decided it might be good for you to go again. So, we all loaded up in the car and went together as a family. When we arrived on the fairgrounds, we parked the car, put you in your wheelchair, and pushed you down the midway to the gate of the bumper car ride.

The ride operator, although uneasy, let us enter, and we loaded you into a car with your dad beside you. I was encouraged as you tried to steer the car with your former aplomb, challenging the other drivers. Unfortunately, the other drivers looked at you strangely and drove away, unwilling to play with you. Frustrated, you got tired of our experiment pretty quickly and wanted off the ride. If the truth be known, I was disappointed, too. I was so hoping you would have a better experience and wished the other drivers on the ride had been more willing to play with you that day.

I remember in past years, once you kids ran out of ride tickets, and after we visited the pigs, cows, chickens, and goats in the animal barn, we'd all head for the food court for chorizo, baked Idaho potatoes, and ice cream. After stuffing ourselves with all the food our stomachs could hold, we'd call it a day and head for the car. All you kids would be clutching cotton candy in your sticky hands. And you, Jeff, would still be full of energy, wishing the evening could go on, but your younger sisters would be drooping, needing to be picked up and carried to the car.

This year, after the bumper cars and the visit to the animal barn, you ate the chorizo, the baked potato, and the ice cream. And you even finished off with the cotton candy. But, this time, it all fell flat. It's like this year was a "shadow fair," an altered experience that came up short compared to past fairs. We were all subdued and saddened as we rolled you back to the car. We had hoped the fair you loved so much before the accident would still be there for you.

When winter arrived and pool therapy ended, your physical

therapist and I came up with another plan. In retrospect, maybe it was a little too ambitious, and a bit ridiculous, but we decided that you might get excited about going skiing. You were once a fearless skier. I remember how you would fly down the hill with abandon, attacking the moguls for lift so you could soar into space, challenging the fall line as you raced to the bottom. So, with the arrival of snow, we arranged a trip to Bogus Basin.

Looking back, I know you weren't very enthusiastic about this activity. You were probably a bit more realistic than us, but you reluctantly went along with our plan. We loaded you onto a sled and pulled you to an open, flat spot. Jill put on her skis, and Larry and I attached you to your skis before taking you off the sled. As we pulled you upright onto the snow, you fought to maintain your balance and said in your flat voice, "I don't think this is a good idea." We persisted, though, encouraging you to simply give it a try.

Jill held your hands while she skied backward with her skis open in a *V* shape. Then, you skied toward her into the *V*, which acted as a brake. But you quickly lost your enthusiasm. I hadn't accounted for the fact that your temperature control wasn't what it used to be before the accident, and you could no longer tolerate the cold. Once we realized what was happening, we quickly removed your skis, loaded you back onto the sled, helped you into the car, and left Bogus Basin.

I can't imagine how frustrating this must have been for you, Jeff. Yet another experiment that hadn't worked. I hope you understand that we tried these things to help you. We were hoping to find something that you would want to do badly enough that you would give it an extra push and, in turn, regain some of your former life.

Soon after we'd brought you home from the Elks, some of your friends called to see how you were doing, so we arranged a dinner with them at a local pizza joint. We all sat around a long wooden table, with the pizzas spread out in front of us and frosty-cold soft drinks in our hands. Your friends tried to make conversation with you. And I could see that they tried to understand your responses. You were speaking, but in your flat monotone, you were hard to understand, and soon they stopped asking questions. There just wasn't that much to talk about. You weren't living a life they could relate to anymore.

There wasn't much laughter at the table that night, just friends trying to hang in there for you. We thought they wouldn't be calling much longer, and predictably, they faded away, one by one. I admired them for trying, these young guys, and understood when they quit. I hope you can understand also, Jeff. Your life is so different from theirs now. They still care about you, and I know they have been trying to find some common ground, something they can do with you. But I have found, in my life, that friendships can't be forced. Common interests must occur naturally. And when those interests are no longer there, most friends simply drift away, as was the case with your friends from school.

Before they stopped calling, we did try to help you reach out to your friends—and also to have more access to family, like your Uncle Bill. To that end, your dad and I decided to put a phone in your bedroom so you could call friends and family. It seemed like a good idea at the time. We thought maybe it would improve your life and give you some control in an otherwise-challenging recovery period. It wasn't long after giving you access to a phone in your room, however, that you showed us how bad an idea that actually was.

I remember the doorbell waking us up in the middle of the night. Your dad and I hastily grabbed our clothes and ran to the front door. Standing on the other side were two policemen, responding to a 911 call for help. They said an "old woman" had made the call. Your dad and I just stood there for a moment before we realized you had made the call. We led them to your room. You told the policemen that you had gotten frustrated and decided to call 911. We apologized to them, and they were very kind and understanding. Unfortunately, we had to remove your phone.

Your dad and I still didn't know how much mental acuity you had retained after the head injury. We wanted to see if you could succeed in school, but we didn't know how or where this might take place. Ever optimistic, we called the school district to see what they could offer and asked if you could return to junior high school. We made an appointment with the principal of your school, and, after our meeting, he said we could enroll you. Your dad and I were hopeful that you could master the subjects and eventually go on to graduate from high school. They said you would have an aid to help you in class, since you couldn't see well enough to read anymore. With the damage to your eyes, you were considered legally blind. Regardless, they put you in both special education and mainstream classes, to see how you would do.

Life sure has some ironic twists and turns, doesn't it, Jeff? I remember getting a phone call last year from your school, just a few weeks before your accident. They had called to complain about your behavior that day. Apparently, you had been teasing one of the special education kids. We punished you back then; now, here you are in class, maybe sitting next to the person you once teased.

Recently, I had a conversation with one of your mainstream teachers: She seems a bit frustrated about having you in her class. She asked me what I am hoping you will get out of being in school. I was a bit stumped by that question, as I really had no big plans when we enrolled you. I mean, I've never been presented with a problem even remotely similar to the one we are now facing. What should I expect, given your severe head injury?

I've read the stories. It's inspiring to hear about someone who miraculously wakes up and recovers one day, and then goes on to Harvard. I cling to those stories, although I think that opportunity has passed for us. They still give me some hope, but it doesn't seem that you're quite on that trajectory.

Your dad and I now have no thoughts of a miracle recovery, but we aren't sure how much of your previous life you can regain. Maybe you can come back far enough to have some sort of independent life. That's what we are hoping. That's why I didn't really have an answer for your teacher. We simply don't know.

What I really want for you is to not have a head injury or psychological problems. I'd also like it if you could see well, walk without stumbling, and not speak in a monotone that's challenging to understand. I guess I haven't really thought this all through, Jeff. For now, I think I just want you to eventually graduate from high school, as a first step to whatever lies ahead for you.

To that end, I usually try to help you with your homework. We sit in a built-in study area in your room, your books on the counter, our two chairs together as we try to work through your assignments. I always knew teaching would not be my profession, and you put it succinctly when you said in your monotone voice, "Don't ever be a teacher, Mom." Your words gave me a lift as I smiled at your perception. Good advice, indeed.

I wasn't that surprised when your teacher asked to speak with me. Jeff, you get so frustrated and you're so impulsive. You can be a danger to yourself and others. There was another incident in school recently. You got so upset that you rolled your wheelchair off the auditorium stage, crashing several feet below. Luckily, you didn't hurt yourself badly, but it certainly shook up the teachers and other students. I know just how fast you can do something like that, so I don't blame the school. I don't think they were at fault.

And just the other day, I was in the kitchen preparing dinner. You were near me sitting on a stool at the counter. The girls were a few feet away watching TV. Suddenly, you grabbed the large knife I had been using, and it took all my strength to wrestle that knife away from you without either one of us getting hurt. The poor girls! They thought you were trying to hurt me. I was more concerned that you were trying to hurt yourself.

As I stood there shaking, I thought to myself how much you would hate having me go through this. We just don't know what you're thinking sometimes, Jeff, but I know you. You have always been very protective of me, and I know how much the Jeff before the accident would detest witnessing these incidents.

Every once in a while, your dad and I just need to get away for an evening. But we can't leave you home with the girls and a sitter. So, we contacted a nursing home, and they agreed to let you occasionally stay there overnight. Unfortunately, late one evening, they called to report an incident.

You were not cooperating when it was time to go to bed. One of the staff members had decided the best plan was to tie you down. (They were not trained to deal with head injuries.) You struggled, grabbed the call bell, and swung it around, hitting the attendant in the eye. I don't think the nursing home acted wisely at all, but we can't have you hurting people in your frustration. That's one resource fewer in our town to help us care for you. Whatever are we going to do, Jeff? We keep trying to find a path that will let our family live a more-or-less-normal life and keep you safe and happy. But we keep running out of options.

Your dad and I have not given up on your vision. You can see better with your left eye, but it's tilted and you can't open and close your eyelid. So, we took you to our ophthalmologist to see if he had any suggestions. He thought that, maybe, a specialist he knew in San Francisco could perform surgery to straighten it, fix your eyelid, and give you better vision overall. So, our ophthalmologist sent your records off. And after the specialist looked them over, we booked a flight to San Francisco.

Traveling on a plane with you is tense business, Jeff. We never know when you are going to get upset and throw your drink or have some other outburst. Fortunately, we managed to get there with no major problems, but our nerves were stretched pretty thin. Once we arrived, we met with the eye surgeon and, unfortunately, after he examined you, he said there was no hope of success. You, of course, were very upset and disappointed. We tried to comfort you as one more hope faded away.

Disappointed, we returned to the airport and waited for another tense flight. Once we were settled in at the terminal, I left you and your dad to go to the restroom. As I walked out of the restroom, I stopped and looked around for just a moment. . . . I was anonymous in that large airport. I could have walked away, merged into the crowd of strangers, and simply disappeared into the city. The idea was strangely seductive, but only a random, fleeting desire to escape.

I took a deep breath, pulled myself together, and returned to you and your dad. Walking toward you and Larry, I thought about getting through the return airplane trip—and then reminded myself that we would all soon be home again, with your sisters. I wonder if your dad has ever hit a wall with this situation; if he's had similar thoughts. I wouldn't blame him at all if he did. I know that sounds terrible, but we have our limits, too, Jeff.

Speaking of which, I worry that I am reaching a breaking point. After yet another difficult outburst from you, Jeff, I grabbed your empty wheelchair and pushed it with all my strength into the fireplace. I know that's crazy behavior, but this simply can't go on! You are not doing well with us at home. In fact, your behaviors seem to be escalating and getting more dangerous for all of us.

I'm certainly not able to cope as well as I did when you first came back home almost a year ago. I know it won't help matters if I become completely unhinged, Jeff. And I seem to be losing it. After many long discussions and lots of tears on my part, your dad and I have come to the conclusion that none of us can go on like this.

So, we've done some research and found a resource that might be able to help us. We took the first step and called the National Association for the Head Injured for suggestions. We're at our wit's end here, Jeff, and need to figure out a better way to care for you. We realize now that caring for you is more than the family alone is able to handle. We clearly need help.

Well, it's growing late. Funny how time passes when I sit down to write these letters to you. You're already asleep in your room, hopefully for the night. Your dad and the girls are also in bed. I'd better stop writing this letter and try and get some sleep, too.

Good night, my son. Sleep well.

Letter 9

Oakland Rehabilitation Facility

Well, Jeff, I can't believe it has been six months since you moved from home to the Oakland Rehabilitation Facility in Texas. Suffering through all the ramifications of your accident seems to just get harder and harder for all of us. I hate being separated from you by thousands of miles. It was such a hard decision to, once more, turn your care over to the experts in hopes that something could be done to improve your condition, both mentally and physically. There is, again, a big empty space in this house. When you are not here, we are incomplete; the family unit is missing an integral part. But what do you do when that part must be repaired?

We considered several options when we realized that we needed help caring for you. We wanted you to remain in the West, so we had tentatively ruled out any place east of the Rockies. Even so, we found several facilities in Texas, as well as California, and spent time on the phone interviewing all of them. After our discussions with all of the various rehabilitation facilities, your dad and I narrowed it down to a few places in Texas. One of them stood out to us; it was located on several acres in the countryside, an hour or so from Austin. Your dad and I decided that we wanted to visit it first, so we flew out to Texas.

After we landed in Austin, we rented a car and drove to the Oakland facility. Our first impression was very positive. As we wound our way up the drive, we saw a ranch house and several outbuildings with corrals, where the animals were housed. As we walked toward the ranch house to meet with the managers, we noticed several people (residents, we later learned) working with the animals.

On that trip, we discovered that Oakland Rehabilitation Center is owned by a father and son. The father is a psychiatrist, and his son works as the administrator. We found them very engaging, especially the son. They shared their philosophy with us, which is based on behavior modification. That sounded right to us, Jeff. We knew that your behavior must be modified if you were to be successful in living a more normal life.

While we were there, they gave us copies of testimonials written by parents whose children had been miraculously transformed under their care. They candidly stated that they'd had great luck with some individuals, and that there were others they just couldn't help at all. During our discussion, we did not get the impression that you would automatically be accepted. They seemed very reluctant to accept anyone, unless they believed the candidate would be a good fit for their program. We were, therefore, very hopeful when they agreed to have a representative come to Boise and evaluate you, Jeff.

I remember, when we returned home and described the scene at Oakland to you, how excited you were at the possibility of going to live on a ranch in Texas. You always were one to embrace change, and that worried me. I was hoping that you also understood what this change meant—that you would be living away from Idaho and your family for an indefinite period of time. Within a month, Brian, the representative from Oakland, had arrived. You tried really hard and made a good effort, showing Brian all the progress you had already made. You even walked in the front yard without assistance for about 40 yards, before losing your balance. You also answered all his questions, to show him you could process information and have a real conversation.

Your behavior was very appropriate during the visit. Soon after Brian returned to Texas, we were notified that you had been accepted at Oakland! You really seemed to want this, so we were very happy for you, Jeff. We made arrangements for you, your dad, and I to fly to Austin. Once we got there, we rented a car and all made the short trip to Oakland. We had planned to spend several hours there with you, but that did not happen. When we arrived, they greeted us and got you settled into your bunkhouse—and then we were expected to leave. We drove back to Austin with very mixed feelings: We didn't like leaving you so abruptly and had hoped to visit a little longer with the staff. It certainly caught us by surprise that there would be none of that.

Your dad and I spent that night in a hotel in Austin. We lay in bed, stiff with a mixture of anxiety and sadness, with hopes and fears. Our minds squirreled around, trying to see if there were any other options for continuing to work with you at home. We had gone through this process dozens of times before we made the decision to seek outside help in caring for you, Jeff. And we always arrived at the same conclusion. Idaho did not have the resources needed to help us care for you at home or in a facility. Your dad spent that night dry-eyed and sleepless, whereas I tossed and turned, with tears streaming down my cheeks, until I finally fell into a restless sleep. The next day we returned to Boise, simultaneously wondering if we had made a mistake and what, if anything, we could do about it.

*　*　*

Life can change so quickly, Jeff. It seems like such a short time ago that the three of us made that trip to Boise to start our life together, after your dad and I got married. You were such a cute little guy and always on the move. Our first house was a bit tight for an energetic little boy. It was a two-bedroom house with about 800 square feet, which you probably don't even remember, since you were only two years old.

Our house had a nice fenced backyard for you to play in and a terraced garden for me to grub around in. Do you remember the two ducks that showed up that summer? They practically lived with us. I remember how they liked to get into your little plastic pool and splash around. Whenever I think back on those early days in Boise, I smile when I picture my little boy trying to play with those ducks.

Back then, your dad worked within walking distance of our home. In nice weather, we would walk down the street to meet him on his way home for lunch. After lunch, I would put you down for a nap, which you usually refused to take. You wanted to be on the go, running after the ducks, riding your little tricycle on the front sidewalk, or getting out your toys to play.

But I was tired and needed you to take a nap so the housework could get done. It was no use: You were always a force to be reckoned with.

We only lived there for a couple of years before we moved to a larger home in a typical subdivision. We thought we needed a larger place, because we expected our family to grow. Your grandmother had taken to phoning me frequently to point out that I was getting a bit old for childbirth and should not delay if we wanted to have more children. I was only 25 and therefore a bit surprised at this uncharacteristic nagging on her part. Given my "advanced age," we took her advice, and soon we had a new little sister for you. Amy arrived with a dusting of red hair on her head and looking a lot like a Cabbage Patch doll. We have some cute pictures of the two of you. In one photo, your arm is encircling the infant carrier, and you and Amy are looking into each other's eyes, taking each other's measure. Within a year, you had another baby sister. Pam had sparse blonde hair and big blue eyes. *One more girl baby*, you must have thought. Even so, you liked her from the get-go.

A year or two after the girls arrived, Larry filed the adoption papers and officially became your dad. You hadn't had much contact with your biological father since he'd moved to California. He came to Idaho once or twice to visit you. And you only made one trip to California to visit him and his wife and two kids.

That visit must have been hard for you, Jeff. It couldn't have been easy seeing your biological father with different kids and a different wife. I'm sure you felt like a stranger within their family; you never asked to go there again. When we approached Tom about Larry adopting you, he gave his consent. We were relieved, as Larry had effectively been your dad for several years.

With the formal adoption, he became your dad legally, and I felt more secure. Our little family was united as one.

My relationship with your grandpa also changed during these years. Of course, my dad was the same man he had always been, but with my transformation from a disappointing child into the bride of a lawyer, he seemed to want a better relationship. You might ask why I was willing to accept the new approval, and it would be a good question. I guess the short answer is that every girl wants and needs the love of a father, even when there is a risk of further hurt. So my dad and I chose to ignore the past and move forward. Now, I make chili with him; I continue loving my mother, as before; and your dad and I take trips with both of my parents. The four of us seem to enjoy being together as adults.

You just know your grandpa as he is today—sort of a difficult, caustic person. But he was once a young man just starting off in the world, like you. After what he describes as a turbulent childhood with cold, demanding parents, he was finally ready to begin his own journey. I don't think I ever shared this story with you, but my dad decided to go to college right after graduating from high school. He left immediately, heading for the highway to catch a ride—north, to the University of Idaho, or south, to Utah State.

The Good Samaritan who stopped and picked him up happened to be heading north. Such is fate, I suppose. If he had found a ride to Utah State, none of us would be here. Gives you pause for thought, doesn't it, Jeff? Anyway, it turned out that my dad didn't stay in college for very long. The war came along, and he dropped out to serve his country. At least that is the story we've been led to believe.

Later revelations seem to indicate that the university dropped him, informing him that he was no longer welcome. Looking back, I can imagine that he would be a difficult person to have in class. He often talked about the ignorant professors he encountered while attending college. In any event, he got a real break when he met your grandmother. They fell in love, and she agreed to marry him. I can't imagine any other woman making that relationship work. That was in 1942. With war sabers rattling, he soon enlisted in the navy. As luck would have it, he never saw battle. After basic training, the navy ordered him to attend school, where he was trained as an electrician. After that, he was assigned to a naval base at Oak Harbor, Washington. Fortunately, he was able to serve his country in wartime without ever seeing the enemy.

As I said, the navy trained your grandpa to be an electrician. And that was his job for many years, until he decided to get his real estate license. In spite of his honesty and intelligence, real estate didn't work out very well for him. You also need a bit of patience, charm, and tact to be successful in that business, all three of which my dad lacked. I don't suppose things were going too well financially in our household at that time, either, but kids don't always know about those types of things. In any event, he stumbled onto something else, something that would provide a very good living and also fit his unique personality and skill set.

Shortly after you were born, your grandpa bought a bar in our little college town. He turned that little bar into a thriving college hangout that was standing room only on weekends. He had finally found his niche. And he had good business sense; he understood that the money in the till isn't income until all the expenses have been covered. He also knew that he had to be present every day to run the business successfully. And, maybe most surprising, the college kids were crazy about him.

Your grandpa really liked being around college kids, especially if they were majoring in something he considered worthwhile, such as engineering, law, or accounting. I think the college kids liked him because of his caustic wit, intelligence, and remarkable memory. His brain was like an encyclopedia. The kids would discuss their subjects with him, and often he had answers or insight to provide. They didn't seem to mind his verbal stingers, either. A few glasses of beer would soften the sting of his words, leaving his wit to shine through. And he was generous. He'd been known to help out kids who needed financial aid for tuition or books.

My dad didn't have a great relationship with his parents. He didn't provide us with much information, but I remember him saying that his mother was a shrew and his dad, an ineffectual provider. Dad didn't encourage dialogue when he made his pronouncements. I also know that he considered them prejudiced. He said that when he was a kid, growing up in the country in southern Idaho, they forbade him to play with the kids of the Mexican migrant workers—or even to walk with them to and from the school bus. This was one of many things that he resented from his childhood. I have always wondered if that was why he named me, his firstborn, Carmen. This more typically Hispanic name might have been a poke in the eye to his parents.

My poor dad wasn't allowed to have much of a childhood. His family lived on a hardscrabble farm, which barely allowed them to eke out an existence. His dad had been a schoolteacher; I am not sure why he left teaching. So his family tried to make a living on that small farm, which Dad always said wasn't productive enough to adequately support them. In addition to growing crops, they had a few cows, and he had to come home right after school and care for them. He claims he was a pretty fair tennis player in high school, and I don't doubt it, because he never exaggerates his accomplishments. He wanted to practice after school and compete, but he wasn't allowed to because of his chores. When *we* were little kids, he always insisted that we be allowed to play. Oh, we had a few chores, but he also wanted us to have a childhood, and that included allowing us more time for play than he'd had.

You remember your great-grandparents, Jeff. When we moved to southern Idaho, we saw more of them, because they lived about an hour away. I always thought my dad's parents to be loving and kind grandparents. My grandma had pure white hair. I never saw it any other color. Even when she was around 50 years old, she looked like a little old lady, with her frail build, rayon housedresses, and fine, white cotton-candy hair. My grandpa, whom Dad called *The Ranger*, was also thin. He was of medium height and a bit stooped. He had a fine intellect and told a good story. They usually invited us over for Sunday dinner. When we arrived, my grandma, Mary, would already have a pot roast, complete with carrots and potatoes, roasting in the oven. And you always enjoyed her cookies. I can still picture her bending over with the plate so you could take one. I don't know if you remember—they had a small yard where you could run around while I helped her get dinner on the table.

Your dad and my grandpa usually sat visiting in the living room whenever we would stop by. I remember my grandpa explaining to him, once, about why he helped promote the graduated income tax years before. He expressed regret over his actions. He said the graduated income tax was sold to the public on the basis that it would only affect the rich, whomever that might be. In practice, these political promises never seem to work out quite like the voters expect.

* * *

Many decisions that seem good at the time don't work out as expected in the long run. Oakland was one of those decisions, Jeff. You should always pay attention to the little warning signs. Sometimes, they are so subtle that they don't even break through to conscious thought when you first see them.

When your dad and I initially toured Oakland, I noticed the residents didn't meet our eyes. Instead, their eyes shifted away nervously as we went by. It didn't really register then. For one thing, they all had head injuries, so I couldn't expect them to react in a typical manner. And we were quickly taking it all in, looking here and there at the ranch, petting the small animals, talking with the staff members, thinking about how much you would love the setting, and so on. It was just a small, slightly off-key note, which got lost in the larger performance.

And so, you continued your rehabilitation at Oakland. When we left, we were told that we should not contact you for a few weeks. They said they wanted you to settle into your new environment, and the psychiatrist warned that our phoning you during this process would interfere.

It wasn't long, however, before they were calling us. They said you were not adjusting well to the behavior modification program. I was horrified when they said you were starting to self-mutilate. Since you don't have any sensation on one side of your face, that was where you inflicted the damage. While you were there, you were so distraught that you tore your eyelid, which had to be surgically repaired. And you've continued to harm yourself, tearing your eyelid a few more times over the past several months.

Your dad and I wondered what was going on, so we scheduled a trip to Texas to personally check out your situation. While we were there, however, you seemed fine. There were no outbursts. There was no drama. Even your balance and endurance seemed to have improved. We all walked around together to see where you slept, exercised, and ate your meals. We were told about your activities and met more of the staff. When it was time for us to leave, you were sitting in the dining room with the other residents, eating your dinner. You didn't seem to take much interest in the fact that we were leaving. I turned around to have another look as you bent your head over your plate. I was surprised at your lack of emotion, but I was simultaneously relieved that you were so calm.

As you know, Christmas is a big deal in our family, and we just couldn't imagine having it without you. Months before, we coordinated your trip home with the staff at Oakland. They agreed to arrange for you to be accompanied by a staff member. We were all so excited that you would be able to come home for Christmas. We carefully purchased your gifts and made plans for the week that you would be there. Just before your flight, however, we were told that you would not be allowed to come home due to your recent behavior. You were still resistant to behavior modification.

I want you to know that we argued the point, but they said that your staying there instead of coming home was not negotiable if you were to remain a resident at Oakland. I was very upset by this decision. I knew how disappointed you would be to miss this trip, too, and I couldn't face Christmas thinking of you, in Texas, wanting so badly to be at home with your family. I just couldn't quit fretting and worrying.

So your dad, hoping to divert my attention, asked me if I wanted to go up north to my parents' house. *Yes*, I thought, *let's do that*. I couldn't stand to be in our house without you, Jeff. I called my mom and told her what had happened—and that we were thinking about coming to stay with them for Christmas. She warmly encouraged us to make the trip. And so we started the snowy ride through the mountains, bringing the girls, the presents, and, of course, our heavy hearts with us.

Unfortunately, things haven't improved since that horrible Christmas. In the weeks that followed, your dad and I started to think that something wasn't right about Oakland, Jeff. There were just too many things ringing alarm bells. For one thing, the psychiatrist told me over the phone that you tearing your eye "sickened him." That caused the alarm bells in my head to ring even louder. What an insensitive comment for a professional in charge of severely head-injured clients to make. Then, I remembered the shifting, nervous eyes of the clients when we first toured the facility. And then your surprisingly detached demeanor as we were leaving, a couple of months ago. We became totally disillusioned with Oakland.

Well, today we got a surprising call from them. Apparently, they don't think you are suited to be a client there, either. While it came as quite a shock, part of me is relieved. Finally, we are in perfect agreement with the folks at Oakland! I'm so sorry this didn't work out, Jeff. After only six months, we need to make another change. Your dad and I are putting everything else aside until we get this figured out. We'll be in touch as soon as we know what our next steps are going to be.

I just looked up at the clock, and it is very late, yet again. I hope someday I can have these conversations with you in person, instead of writing letters that you most likely will never read. We are counting heavily on rehabilitation working a miracle, while we know in our hearts that time is not on our side. With every month that passes, they say there is less of a chance that you will improve any more than you already have. For now, these letters are the best means I have for communicating my thoughts. Good night, my son.

Letter 10

Greenwood Schools

Dear Jeff,

I am sitting here in my living room, reflecting on how time just keeps marching on, with no regard for the huge disruption you have experienced in your young life. You living in Texas has become the new normal. While I am grateful we were able to find another facility for you and get you out of Oakland relatively quickly, I have trouble getting my head around the fact that you are so far away, even if Greenwood seems to be a better fit for you.

Meanwhile, I continue to go to college and will soon graduate. Can you believe it, Jeff? And the girls are growing up and pursuing new activities. They both joined the school band and are now playing the clarinet. Amy started junior high and has taken quite an interest in her science class. Pam has really taken off with her horseback riding—and has outgrown her pony. We need to get her a new horse. Your dad goes to work and continues to build his law practice. And as I write this letter, my mind drifts back to when we first moved to the country. How happy you kids were to be country kids.

Your sisters used to wear the cutest little dresses to school when we lived in town. After the first week or so in the country school, however, they announced that they wanted to wear jeans. They said that they were now country girls. And, of course, in addition to jeans, country girls needed horses, which fortunately had already been our plan.

You may not remember watching your dad and I suffer through the pitfalls of horse hunting. At the time, you were busy adjusting to a new school and making new friends in our little six-acre-lot subdivision. When we decided to move to the country, we committed to getting a trail bike for you and some horses for the girls. Although we grew up close to farm life, neither one of us knew anything practical about horses.

With no knowledge or experience to draw from, we consulted some "experts." Our neighbor Jim's advice was concise and clear: "No ponies. They are evil-tempered animals that like to inflict damage on young and old." He thought a well-trained mare, about eight or nine years old, would be the best choice. Our second advisor, a grouchy old man who lived a little farther down the road, said only a fool would match a small child to a large horse. His advice was to get a very young, small pony, which could be trained right along with the child.

Armed with this conflicting information, we consulted the classifieds and looked at many horses. One gelding, advertised as a child's horse, was said to be fine, so long as you didn't mind him rearing when he was unhappy—which was only when he was being ridden. The next horse we looked at certainly wasn't dangerous: She wouldn't move at all. This was because she was getting over distemper and had no energy. Suffice it to say, we were beginning to get discouraged. The odds of our recognizing a suitable horse for our young girls were not looking good.

Luckily, we ran into Sylvia. You probably remember her, Jeff. She used to come by and pick up the girls and take them to 4-H shows. She also raised POAs (Ponies of the Americas), and somewhere along the line, she was recommended as a good source for kids' horses. POAs seemed to be about the right size, just under standard horses—and somewhere in between the recommendations we had gotten. So, under Sylvia's guidance, we ended up with a gelding named Dusty, for Pam, and a mare named Lightfoot, for Amy.

Do you remember them, Jeff? All this happened just before the accident. Well, Lightfoot turned out to be in foal and gave us a beautiful little colt that Amy named Blazer. Dusty, Pam's little pony, is a little ornery, which, I'm sure you'll agree, is a fairly good match for Pam. They both like to gallop. Whenever I'd peek out the window, I'd often see Dusty's dark mane and tail flowing and Pam's blonde pigtails bouncing.

Since your dad and I were clueless about training horses, we had the girls join a nearby 4-H club. And since the horses needed transportation to get to all the horse shows, it didn't take long before we discovered that we also needed a horse trailer—and then, of course, a big pickup truck to pull that trailer.

This project is getting more and more complicated. At least the girls are becoming good little riders and have started showing their horses at small venues, so I guess it's worth the extra effort. When your dad and I go to a horse show, we sidle up to the arena, lean on the fence, and try not to look like city folk. We always wear jeans, but I don't think we are fooling anyone.

We recently took the girls to one of the local shows. We were watching from the bleachers when a horse got spooked and reared. It slipped and landed on the leg of the young boy rider. I was concerned, of course—but my main thought was that legs can be fixed. It didn't appear that he had a head injury. So, I settled back in, thinking all must be well.

Do you remember when you insisted that I go riding with you and Eric on his family's horses? That turned out to be quite a day, didn't it? We decided it would be safer for me to ride off-road, rather than on the pavement, to provide a fairly soft landing in case I fell. All went well until Eric's horse decided to wade into the pond and mine was determined to follow. I pulled on the reins. I tried to turn his head and drummed my heels into his side, but there was nothing I could do to control the beast. There we were, horses side by side, with nothing but squishy mud under us. I could feel the horses sliding toward each other while they sank deeper into the mud. I could see that if they sank further, I might be caught between them.

In a split second, I had to make a decision. I threw myself off the back of the horse and into the pond. I maneuvered through the mud and water and managed to get out. Meanwhile, Eric and the horses had also left the pond. As I stood there dripping, shivering, and just a bit annoyed, you were busy pummeling Eric for trying to kill me. Although I shouted at you, demanding that you cease and desist beating on poor Eric, I privately admired your sweet and protective attitude toward me.

While it is pretty common for me to lecture you kids about your behavior, I have now taken to lecturing perfect strangers. For example, the other day I was driving down a busy street. I noticed a pickup on the road next to me, and the bed was loaded with young guys behaving with the usual disregard for personal safety that teenage boys often have. They turned into a parking lot, and I followed them in. I then gave them a long lecture on what the consequences would be if they managed to fall out of that pickup. I got rather graphic, too, and they were looking pretty somber by the time I got back into my car. Of course, tears were rolling from my eyes as I explained about head injuries. I hope my words made a difference. Life can change forever in a split second, and most young people don't seem to have that awareness.

I've noticed that I may be getting a bit more grouchy and short-tempered lately. College requires many hours of stuffing things into my brain that I am basically uninterested in. Why in the world did I settle on accounting, for heaven's sake? I have always disliked math! But I was trying to be practical, darn it. I did wander through the business majors before settling on accounting; to my surprise, that was my strongest area.

I started in finance, but there were way too many formulas we had to memorize. Economics had too many statistics classes. Computer science required me to be very precise, and there was no way to find my errors, except by painstakingly studying endless lines of code. I was totally uninterested in marketing and management, so there I was in accounting. And it did make sense to me, in a way. I always liked arranging things, so the flow from income statements to balance sheets was satisfying.

But, on top of my classes, I run a household with a husband and two busy girls. Did I mention that your sisters are taking dance lessons? Their classes are in town. To get them to their lessons on time, I have to race home after class and grab the girls off the bus. We're so pressed for time that they change in the car on our way. Once they start their lessons, I head for the building's basement and try and get some homework done. We then race home so I can put some kind of meal together.

I usually start that process by throwing down a cup of instant coffee (no time to brew) for the caffeine lift. Between your dad and I, we get the girls going on their own homework. Eventually, I head for the study and try and prepare for the next day of classes. Weekends are devoted to all the different activities your sisters are involved in, plus the usual gardening, laundry, and mucking out the house. Things are carrying on at a fast clip, but each semester, I tell myself that I can do anything for four months. And when this semester comes to an end, I will have a shining degree and finally be a college graduate—in accounting, no less! That will be a special moment.

Just before your accident, you and I had a special moment, Jeff. At least it was for me. It was a beautiful evening, and we were in the backyard, enjoying the sunset. I remember we were looking up at the sky, hoping to spot our resident white owl. The sun had set, but there was still a glow where it hadn't quite slipped over the edge of the earth into darkness. Sure enough, the white owl flew into sight—on command, one might think—to start his nightly prowl. As he skimmed above the pool, its lights revealed his beautiful white coloring. I had my arm around your shoulder and, as you leaned against me, you said in a hushed voice, "Isn't this beautiful?" My heart was warmed by the fact that my rambunctious, insensitive teenage boy had such reflections tucked away inside of him.

Now, I am not sure what is going on in your head. Now that the Jeff we once knew is gone, I am trying to understand this new Jeff. I have no expectation that you will return to your previous mental and emotional states: The brain damage from the accident is too severe. But I do hope you have some beautiful thoughts you can bring to the surface. We keep hoping that, somehow, rehabilitation will be the miracle that restores your body to a level where you can be independent, someday. Although we don't say it, I think your dad and I both fear that you will never return home and resume the life you lived before the accident. That possibility probably dwindled away during the two years after your accident. But we continue to hope for a better life than this for you, and recently, our hope has rested in the hands of the staff at Greenwood.

We were so lucky to find Greenwood right at the time we needed to remove you from Oakland. At Greenwood, they never even mention the now-hated term "behavior modification." Compared to Oakland, Greenwood has an almost clinical atmosphere, which is more functional than it is appealing. Their focus is rehabilitation, as you are very well aware, since you attend several rehabilitation classes each day.

Yet, I am still aggrieved that Oakland didn't live up to its promise and that it wasn't the safe and wonderful place we'd believed it to be. You could have been so happy on the ranch, with the animals and the outdoor space for your therapies, if only their focus and methods had been different. You will have to excuse my ridiculous mental gymnastics. That's like saying hell would be a very nice place to live—if it weren't for the heat, the management, and the occupants. I don't know if you heard, but the state closed down Oakland. I don't know what caused the closure. I'm just glad you were safely gone when it happened.

Greenwood may be a bit understated in atmosphere, but the staff is very professional and kind. And it has been so much easier for us to come visit you, because we can now book a suite on-site. The family quarters were unexpected, as we did not have that benefit at Oakland, and they are very functional. Your dad and I have a bedroom with a bath; you have a bedroom and wheelchair-accommodating bath with shower; and there's a joint living room, where we can all watch movies together in the evening. The kitchen is a common space, shared among multiple suites.

With your escape from the behavior-modification nazis, your behavior has improved significantly. You are now considered safe to be with us overnight, without staff supervision. We can settle into our space and really enjoy being together as a family. The common kitchen, however, is another story. I don't feel very comfortable when we are all in there, preparing and eating our meals with other head-injured residents, who may or may not be with their families. I understand you and your behaviors fairly well. But I don't always feel safe around the other residents, especially when there are no staff members present.

Our last visit to Texas was very interesting, Jeff. As you may know, Greenwood also has a building where they treat young people with psychological issues. Do you remember that large grassy area between the two buildings? When we visited with you earlier this spring, we all went outside, since it was such a nice day. And your sisters are 12 and 13 now, so they get restless when they're cooped up inside for too long. Their eyes widened when they saw a bunch of kids playing volleyball on the grass. They wanted to play, too. We checked with our staff liaison, and he thought it would be okay if the girls joined them.

The players didn't have head injuries, but the group was being treated for psychological issues. They appeared to be like any teenage group playing a hotly contested game of volleyball. So you, your dad, and I settled back to enjoy the game and watch Amy and Pam join in the fun.

The girls fit in just fine, being used to a good rough-and-tumble game. As you know, your sisters are pretty athletic. You helped shape them that way. But they've also been on the swim team; they muscle around their horses in 4-H shows; and now they have dance lessons, which require more physical strength than many people think.

During the game, the volleyball was served from the other side and went long. Amy was running after it, when the staff and players all starting screaming at her to stop. You probably couldn't see this, but the ball had come to rest next to a guy sitting under a tree. A staff member ran over and cautiously retrieved the ball and led Amy away. Do you remember him explaining that the guy sitting under the tree could be very unpredictable and dangerous to approach?

This incident brought us all back to reality. This was not just a group of kids playing volleyball, but a group of young people who needed to be locked up in a psychological facility for their own sake and the sake of others. Your sisters are so young to be learning these hard life lessons, Jeff. Unfortunately, they started learning these lessons a few years ago, with your accident.

I'm grateful that we haven't had any problems bringing you home for visits from Greenwood. They always manage to accommodate us by providing a nice staff person to travel with you. And your Christmas trip didn't cause a crisis this time, thank heavens. We racked our brains to find just the perfect gift for you, something that would add to the quality of your life, since there are so many things you can no longer do. So, your dad came up with the notion of getting you an ATV.

Christmas morning held the same excitement that it always does for our family, but this one was a bit more special. When you came out into the living room in your pajamas, holding onto the railing, you raised the eyelid of your good eye and saw the big ATV—and you almost couldn't believe it was real. Our hearts were so full, finally seeing you excited about something. Unfortunately, an Idaho Christmas is not the time to be driving around the yard on an ATV, so that pleasure was deferred until the summer. But it gave you hope, Jeff. You now had something to really look forward to.

And summer finally arrived! Once again, you were able to travel home with no fuss or bother from Greenwood. As you well know, our second favorite time to gather as a family is on the 4th of July, and we had the usual relatives making the annual pilgrimage to our little ranch in the country. Everyone wanted to be with us when you came home for the holiday.

I remember how much you enjoyed being in the pool on your float. I think you appreciated that you could be part of the fun, just floating around. No balance was required. In that moment, with you just drifting around in the pool, it was like any other 4th of July. The smaller kids were jumping in and out, splashing around. Many of the adults were sitting on the edge, dangling their feet in the water, sipping on gin and tonics, and retelling all the family stories. That evening after dinner, we managed to get most of us into the spa for a warm soak before bed. A couple of the men even helped lower you in so you could be part of the fun. How clear this picture is in my mind. You are squeezed in among all the relatives, snuggling up between your mom and grandma, happy to be back home where you belong.

And best of all, you finally got to ride on your ATV! Jim, a family friend who is a bit younger than the rest of the adults, ran backward across the field for you. You don't see so well anymore, Jeff, and you needed a target, something to focus on, as you drove. Your Uncle Bill ran beside you to help monitor the ride and keep you safe. The rides went on about as long as Jim and Bill could keep up the pace.

Unfortunately, after this visit, some of the shine rubbed off of Greenwood. The unit manager, a woman singularly lacking in charm, scolded us for getting you something you enjoyed while you were home! Her point was that if you had fun when you came home, it made their job more difficult. I find it hard to imagine many situations wherein residents would not prefer their homes to a rehab facility. That fact should have been relatively obvious to someone who had risen to the rank of manager in that field. We chose to ignore her, though, and hope you have had fun each time you've come home for a visit.

While we have been very grateful for Greenwood and the efforts the staff has made to continue your rehabilitation, we always knew there would come a time when they would say that their job was done. Greenwood is not a residential facility; it's a rehabilitation hospital, and they can only keep you there if there's a chance your condition can improve.

Well, recently they called to let us know that you were not improving and would need to seek alternative care elsewhere.

We are now busy looking at the options. We want you to be in a facility where you have a good chance of being happy, with people who are kind—who are dedicated to your well-being as you continue your physical therapy. And, as has been the case all along, that is not possible in Idaho. In fact, we are continuing to investigate other opportunities in Texas.

There was a facility that we were impressed with the first time we considered Texas, a few years ago. Unfortunately, Kaber wasn't accepting residents at the time. It was brand new, located in the Hill Country just west of Austin. We really liked the feel of the building. It has two wings, one for women and one for men—each of which can accommodate eight people, if I remember correctly. There's a nice living room, where families can get together. They also have a family room with a huge TV, where they show movies. The kitchen is open, and they prepare the food right there. They also have animals. There's a nice country back porch, for rocking, talking, and probably spitting—oh, and a pool, with a pop machine close by, which I know you will like.

Your dad and I will be heading for Texas soon, to check out the facility again. We will see if Kaber can provide the type of care you need, and if we think you would be comfortable and happy there. We'll be sure to call once we've made our arrangements to head your way.

Good night, my son.

Letter 11

Kaber Health Care

Well, Jeff, it sure was good seeing you during our last visit. I am so relieved that you were a good fit at Kaber and that we were able to get you transferred from Greenwood so quickly. I understand you have been going to church since you have settled in at Kaber. I've heard stories from the staff that you especially like the after-church social life in the community center. From what I hear, the church ladies are spoiling you with servings of cake, hugs, and general coddling. These stories paint a pretty picture in my mind and give me comfort, since I am not there to spoil you.

I have been going to church again, too. You probably remember that my churchgoing has been a bit haphazard over the years. When the mood struck me, I would load everyone in the car and off we would go in our Sunday best to attend Mass. This dedication would last a few weeks, maybe a few months, and then I would backslide. Once we moved to the country, our churchgoing really fell off.

Do you remember the two churches in our little town? One is a friend's church, and the other is some Bible-thumping protestant denomination. You probably remember that we tried the friend's church for a bit. You liked the youth group, and the girls warbled away in the choir. I sat in the pew a few times, but I got a bit uncomfortable when people started popping to their feet during the service to declare they had the gift of prophesy, or some other gift of the Spirit. It was all very unlike the Catholic Church and definitely out of my comfort zone. Had they started talking in tongues, I probably would have run out the door!

I think I told you that Amy decided to go to the Catholic high school. On her registration form, I put us down as being Catholic. This gives us a break on the tuition, because the parishes financially support the Catholic schools. If we get a tuition break as a Catholic family, it's only right that we support an actual parish.

A couple of my friends spoke highly of a man serving as the parish priest at the cathedral in downtown Boise. So, I made an appointment with him to discuss some issues I have had with the Catholic Church over the years. He listened patiently to my concerns and then said, "I don't have a problem with any of this." Relieved, the girls and I started attending Mass again. We really like the priest, and time will tell if this is where we belong. Since I am so newly reconnected with the Church, I think it is essential that I am comfortable with the priest. If not, I suspect that I will fade away again.

I don't want to nag, but I understand that you have taken

up smoking, Jeff. You know our feelings about smoking, but we know that you need to have something that you enjoy. I also hear, from the staff at Kaber, that you have a special relationship with the owners of a nearby restaurant. In fact, they have two serving sizes of their peach cobbler with ice cream: There is the serving size for the general public and the serving size for Jeff. You seem to be making friends all over the place since moving to Kaber, and that makes me very happy.

We got a phone call from Kaber the other day, to see if we would be willing to pay for you to take piano lessons. We think that is a great idea, Jeff. I hope you enjoy the lessons. You always liked playing an instrument, and I can't wait to hear how all that is going. I know you are continuing with physical therapy to help with your balance and walking skills. I hope you are making use of that pool, too. I remember your other physical therapist said the resistance in the water was great for building muscle mass. Plus, I know how much you like to be in the water.

Your dad and I are so grateful to have found Kaber. It seems to be such a good match for you, Jeff. They have the animals on-site, which you love so much, a pool for relaxation and exercise, games and movies for recreation, and good meals, prepared by the staff right there in their country kitchen.

Yes, I really think this time you are in an excellent place, Jeff. Plenty of staff, good care, and pleasant surroundings. In short, it's all we've been hoping for. Of course, it is very expensive. In fact, it's way beyond our means. Luckily, we have good insurance. You might not know much about insurance, Jeff. You're way too young to even appreciate that problem. When I was your age, most families didn't even have insurance. But back then, the cost of medical care was way more reasonable.

With health insurance now the norm, medical costs have soared. Many people work for large corporations, the state, or the federal government. For them, insurance is provided as a benefit of employment, and the risk is spread among a large population so the premiums are fairly low. When your dad went into private practice, however, we needed to provide our own health insurance. Since we were all healthy, we decided to get a very-high-deductible insurance policy, which would be there for us in case of some catastrophe. This policy had no maximum payout, but the deductible was astronomical.

As you very well know, that disaster did arrive for our family, and we are so relieved that we have such excellent insurance! However, one problem has been causing us some concern. The insurance company keeps raising our rates, along with everyone else's in our small insurance group, I suppose. We don't know how long we will be able to hang on, since the monthly premiums are in the thousands now. If the increases continue, we'll soon be priced out of a policy.

We did get a settlement from your employer's insurance company at the time of your accident, but that was not a huge amount. It's just barely covering our premiums at this point. I know I'm going on about insurance, Jeff, but writing these letters helps me clarify my thoughts. Somehow, putting pen to paper and writing about everything as though I am speaking to you connects us, in my mind, over the miles of our separation. It's also my way of connecting to the Jeff who existed before the accident.

Anyway, I'm beginning to think that the American public has been sold a bill of goods concerning health insurance. Most families running small businesses probably feel complacent because they did the right thing and purchased health insurance. However, they're in for a big shock if they ever need serious help. It seems the insurance companies are only interested in collecting premiums. In my opinion, they have no intention of covering a catastrophic event that continues over time. Should one occur, the insurance company will do whatever they can to get rid of you. Well, I guess we shouldn't dwell on that right now. So far, it's not an immediate problem.

Maybe we can talk about car insurance instead. We had to add on to our policy to cover the girls. Your sisters are driving! Can you believe it? They use the yellow pickup, which has already suffered a lot of bumps and bruises during its lifetime. We figure that's the best vehicle for them, since it's been used pretty hard around our acreage and has suffered a rounded corner or two. Their driving it won't cause us too much heartburn.

They are both good little drivers, actually. They've already been driving for a few years on our property. Since my allergies have gotten so bad, I can't be out when the sage is in bloom anymore. So, we recruited your sisters to drive the pickup while your dad throws hay bales into the back.

I remember when you first started to drive. That same little yellow pickup was in the garage, and you and I were going to run an errand. You begged me to let you back the truck out onto the driveway, insisting you knew how. Against my better judgment, I gave in. You promptly put it in gear and drove it forward, banging into the front wall of the garage. That was its first ding!

I regret how upset I became over that little accident. The pickup was brand new, and I was nervous about your dad's reaction to—first of all—me letting you back it out of the garage and—second of all—you crashing it into the front of the garage. Well, that was a tempest in a teapot, because your dad received the news calmly and didn't holler at anybody. What a guy! Anyway, I'm sorry I was so angry with you that day. It was my mistake. I was the parent, you were the child. I should have just said "no."

But we do have to talk about another situation, Jeff. I got a phone call the other day letting me know about an incident involving you and the police. Apparently, you decided to run away and managed to get off the property at Kaber. We were told that you stumbled up to a neighbor's house, rang the doorbell, and banged on the door. An elderly woman finally answered. When she opened the door a bit and peeked out, she saw you standing there, weaving back and forth, and couldn't understand what you were saying to her. She got scared, slammed the door, and called the police.

I don't understand what you were thinking, Jeff. You can't walk far without falling, and you have nowhere to go, even if you could. You have this wonderful place to live, where they are providing you with everything you need, including genuine affection. Even you can't find anything bad to tell us about Kaber. I know it isn't home, but you weren't happy at home either. Your dad and I want you to give this place a fair chance. You need the care they provide, and they are the best care facility we have found. And it is always wise not to have the police involved in your life. So, please, Jeff, promise me there will be no more running away!

This event with the police shouldn't surprise me, though. I mean, you can be kind of a troublesome kid at times. Do you remember the day that I glanced out the kitchen window and saw you walking home after staying with your friend

Eric overnight? Something wasn't right about your gait, and it caught my attention. The more I watched, the more I thought you resembled a staggering drunk rather than my darling son. So, I decided to investigate.

I met you on the driveway and soon confirmed my suspicion. You confessed to raiding our stash of homemade wine. Your dad and I had been experimenting with several recipes, and the resultant batch had sat there for a year or two, gaining some remarkable potency. Your foray into drinking left you not feeling so good, and you just wanted to crawl into bed and sleep it off. I let you stay in bed for a couple of hours, and then decided a bit of yard work would be good for your soul. So, I roused you, led you outside, and supervised your work—until I took pity on you again and let you go back to bed. As far as I know, you've been able to resist alcohol since that afternoon.

I do have some very unsettling news, Jeff. I just found out that your grandmother has cancer. I'm not sure how serious it is yet, but I'm pretty worried. Apparently, it's something called multiple myeloma. She has an appointment with a specialist in Spokane next week, and we should know more then. I had to worm this information out of your Aunt Laureen.

I knew something was wrong. Your grandmother has been very evasive about things recently. Not anything specific—she just hasn't been communicating like she usually does. Laureen said she didn't want to tell me what was going on because I am in my last semester of college. She didn't want to unsettle me with this news. It was actually worse knowing something was going on and not knowing what it was. But I'm hoping it's not as serious as I'm making it out to be in my mind. We should know more soon, and I'll share the news with you when I can.

Well, I am finally getting to the end of this college business. I'm taking my last three subjects, and all of them are pretty difficult at this point. Soon, I will graduate and start looking for a job. One of my professors is steering me toward auditing. You probably know that accounting was a field I had never considered before going back to college. It is very practical, though, and that is what your dad and I wanted for me. One thing about having a major in accounting is that people tend to think you are smarter than you really are. We shall soon see if that works in my favor when I look for a job.

I hope you will settle in a bit better there, Jeff. I have been worried about you, especially with the recent news about your escape from the facility. Please try and find some pleasure in your days. All the ingredients are there for you to have as good a life as possible at Kaber.

Of course, this is not how we expected or wanted your life to turn out. I don't think anyone can imagine or prepare for the odd twists and turns life can take. Each one of us must grapple with difficulties throughout life, most of them unexpected, and either move on or be stuck in a very difficult place. You have so many people that love you and do all they can to make your life as good as possible. I hope you can find some comfort in that.

We love you very much, Jeff, and I hope to see you soon.

Letter 12

Kaber Health Care

Hi, Jeff. I think we had a nice talk the other day. You were in good spirits and didn't spend the whole conversation trying to make me feel horrible about you being stuck "in that hellhole," as you often describe it. We all want you to be able to live at home, but we also know that it just isn't feasible. You're so emphatic about how miserable you are that I often feel totally dejected when I get off the phone with you.

Sometimes, I call back in five minutes or so, just to make sure you're okay. The staff member who answers usually says something like, "Jeff? No, he's fine. He's sitting out back smoking and telling jokes." Of course, I am very relieved that after we hang up, you aren't melting down into a puddle of grief. However, I can't help but feel like you deliberately try to paint as bleak a picture of your life as possible when we have these phone calls. You apparently save these scenes for me, because your dad and sisters never report such difficult conversations.

I've shared my concerns with the staff at Kaber. They say that many families refuse the phone calls from their head-injured loved ones, because the conversations can be so challenging. I can't bring myself to refuse your calls, but I can certainly empathize with these strangers. At times, I pick up the phone reluctantly, not sure I have the internal strength to face another unpleasant conversation.

I guess my subconscious is working on this as I sleep, to give me renewed strength so I can be available to you when you need to call. I had a dream about you last night. We were in the kitchen. You were my tousle-haired son of maybe 16, and I turned to look at you as if seeing you for the first time in years. In this dream, I asked you if you had any idea what you wanted to be when you grew up. You said, lowering the pitch of your voice, that you thought you might like to be a news broadcaster.

As you walked toward the counter, I noticed that you had a slight limp. I asked about it, and you said you always limped, because the two surgeries on that foot hadn't healed right. I was puzzled. I didn't remember your ever having any surgeries. But since it was a dream, I just accepted it as fact and kept talking to you, wanting to find out more about this other version of you I found in the kitchen. I woke up abruptly, knowing it was just a dream, but I still wanted to talk with you more. But that is not possible. This other Jeff lives, walks, and talks only in my dreams.

I haven't felt the need to sit down and write one of these letters in some time. Life has been going as smoothly as possible, given the circumstances. You've settled in at Kaber, although your phone calls would indicate otherwise. I got a job working as an auditor at the state auditor's office. Your sister Amy is still going to college in Seattle, and Pam graduated from cosmetology school and works in a salon here in Boise. And your niece, Taylor, is such a delight. We get her every Friday, and keep her through the weekend, if Pam needs a bit of a break. Pam has a lot to take care of now, with getting her business built up and taking care of a baby on her own. Your dad and I are doing okay, although something has been messing with my emotional stability, which makes me act a bit weird sometimes.

The first sign of emotional imbalance appeared when I began tearing up during conversations, or while watching commercials that included kids or animals. Sometimes, it seemed I'd tear up for no apparent reason at all. When Amy came home from college at Thanksgiving, we all realized that I wasn't acting like my normal self. We were out and about and then met up with Pam at her salon. While we were at the salon, Amy mentioned she had plans with Pam and some friends, but didn't include me.

Pretty normal stuff, right? Well, as soon as I heard that, I burst into tears, right in front of them and everyone else in the salon! I'm not sure which of us was more startled. Amy turned and, with a puzzled look, suggested that I might want to consult a doctor. I thought that was a good idea, so I did. He ran a test or two and discovered that my estrogen levels had dropped like a rock. This came as a bit of a surprise, as they were normal when I had them tested just a few months ago.

So, the doctor loaded me up on hormones; but I can't say I'm quite back to normal. The other morning, for instance, your dad and I were sitting at the counter eating breakfast. For some reason, at that moment, I decided that your dad was going to leave me for a blonde. Why a blonde, you might ask. I honestly don't know. I guess it's the sort of stuff you think about when your hormones are out of whack.

With tears falling from my eyes, I accused him of this coming betrayal. He put down his cereal spoon, turned, and gave me a searching look. He then asked me to stop by the bookstore and buy him a book or two on menopause, which I agreed to do. Your dad is nothing if not practical and calm in the face of adversity. However, he did share with me later that he was very insulted that, even with my current crazy thinking, I could believe he would do such a thing.

One of the nights Amy was home, we all went out to dinner. It was cold and snowy. Amy and Pam were huddled in their warm clothing in the back seat. I was riding up front with your dad. Suddenly, I was very warm, sweaty in fact. I turned to your dad and said, "I feel so hot. Isn't it hot in here?" Your dad turned to me and said, "Yes, it does feel a bit warm. Let me turn on the air conditioner."

Your poor sisters. They were trapped in the back seat as they struggled to stay warm with the air conditioner blasting freezing air on them—on a cold winter evening, no less. I only realized this later, of course. At the time, I truly believed it was unusually warm in that car. It just goes to show how dedicated your dad is. Had he not read those books on menopause, he might not have understood that I was having a hot flash.

I've come to believe that marriage is a partnership, and one of your dad's jobs is to be the chief financial officer of our relationship. I know I'm the one with the accounting degree, but I don't really like working with numbers. Interestingly enough, this is a fact that I have successfully hidden from my employers. Anyway, Larry likes to build financial statements, and his favorite is a five-year projection of income and expenses. Once a year, he wants to go over it with me, year by year, line by line. I'm usually capable of focusing throughout the 15 to 30 minutes it takes to go through it. But when he brought the statement out the other day for our annual review, I steadied myself for what I knew would be an ordeal.

I tried very hard to pay attention, but the numbers all seemed to swim around. Your dad's lips kept moving, but I couldn't focus on what he was saying. My whole body felt sweaty, which is not unusual for me lately, and my mind just wouldn't work right. Regardless, I made myself stand there and steel through it. I didn't want to let him know that I was incapable of absorbing his well-thought-out plan. It was important to him and our future, after all. I could appreciate that, fortunately, even with my estrogen-starved brain.

About a week later, when we were in bed for the night, he handed me a small box. I wondered what was up. It wasn't my birthday or our anniversary, so I was a little confused. I opened the lid, and nestled inside was a pair of diamond earrings, each with two beautiful, sparkling diamonds. I asked him why he was giving me this wonderful gift, and he said, "Because you are having such a hard time right now." Of course, that brought on more tears! This was maybe the most romantic gift your dad has ever given me. I swear, sometimes I feel like I won the lottery in marrying this man.

Well, your dad is starting to adjust to my periods of unusual behavior, but he is unwilling to risk traveling with me unless I am medically prepared. Before we leave the house for any trip, he always anxiously inquires, "Do you have your hormones?" I then assure him that they are packed, or go back in the house and get them, if need be. You don't need to worry, Jeff. When we come to Texas next time, I'll have my hormones. Your dad will make sure of it.

Our last trip to Texas was great. It was nice of the air force to station Rich and my cousin Terry and their three kids in Austin just at this time. Rich's career with the air force has taken them to many places, but this tour of duty turned out to be very special for our family. In opening up their home to all of us, we've experienced some of our best visits with you in Texas, Jeff. When staying with Rich and Terry, we are all together day and night. It feels more like a family visit when we sleep, eat, and chat in a home, rather than at Kaber or in a motel. And I love it that they visit with you when we can't be there!

I do have to say, though, Texas is kind of a weird state. When Terry picked us up at the airport, we got into the car and she turned on the windshield wipers. The unusual thing was that it wasn't even raining! I've never experienced humidity like that before.

I don't think I mentioned earlier that your grandparents decided to move to Boise. Their home, where my siblings and I grew up and where we have had so many family visits before, is no longer suitable for them. The bedrooms are all upstairs in their Craftsman-style home, and they now want a one-story house. Also, Mom's oncologist is two hours away, and you know how bad the roads can be in northern Idaho in the winter. Plus, Boise has great medical care. As you know, Bob and Laureen and Linda and the girls are here, so it just makes sense for Mom and Dad to move here too.

While I am glad that Mom and Dad will be closer, I find it a bit difficult to give up on the family home. I remember every creak of the stairs; the sound of the porch door slamming as people went in and out; so many meals in the kitchen or the dining room; and the sight of the Christmas tree, with the presents wrapped and waiting for us on Christmas morning. All these memories have been a part of me for decades and are all tied up with our being in that house. Now strangers will live there, filling it with their furniture and making their own memories. To prepare myself, I took the time to mentally walk through the whole house, room by room, and then I imagined letting it go.

I remember when I first saw the house. I was nine, and for all nine of those years, we had lived across town in a small two-bedroom place that my parents bought when Dad returned from the navy. It had a wooden foundation, a small kitchen, a living room, and two small bedrooms. Let's just say it was very *cozy*. When your Aunt Linda came along, it was still serviceable. However, when Janet was born, we ran out of space.

So, your grandparents started looking for houses; and I was excited to be deemed old enough to tag along with them. After much searching, they narrowed it down to two places. One was a three-bedroom ranch-style home with a family room. It was newer and modern—and very functional. The second choice was the Craftsman house, set on a fairly large corner lot. There was a sidewalk leading to the front steps of the house. I remember feeling very grand climbing up those steps onto a wraparound porch that led to the front door. I could almost picture the house's original occupants (from the early 1900s) sitting out there in the summer, on a Sunday after church, receiving any neighbors who happened to call. The man of the house would have worn a brimmed hat and suspenders. The wife would be in a pleated cotton dress with a cinched-in waist.

I remember when we went through the front door, we saw an L-shaped staircase going up to the second floor. On the left were French doors that led into the front room. Another set of French doors separated the front room from the dining room. When we first saw the house, I knew that this front room had to have been called the parlor. There was a stand holding an old Bible, and up against the front window was an uncomfortable looking settee, suitable for visiting with the minister whenever he called. I figured, given his station in life, the minister wouldn't be kept on the porch, but instead ushered into the parlor.

As we walked through the house, my imagination followed. I took in the high ceilings in each room, and I noticed the dining room had an oil stove in the corner that provided heat to the lower level. The kitchen was large and had room for a table suitable for a family of seven. The cabinets were old fashioned and painted white. Off of the kitchen was a pantry with storage and a door that opened onto a steep staircase, leading down to a creepy, cold basement. As I peeked down those stairs, I didn't think I would ever want to spend any time down there. The kitchen had a door opening onto a good-sized back porch. There was a door from the porch that led to the backyard and a driveway with a single-car garage.

There were four bedrooms upstairs, one of which had served as a den for the previous owners. It had floor-to-ceiling bookshelves, a large desk, and a pot stove. In my mind, I pictured the former owner cozy and warm while sitting next to the pot stove. He would have been paying the bills, maybe while enjoying a stiff shot of whiskey to ease the blow of having to spend his money. I liked that each of the bedrooms had a large closet that ran the length of the room, with a light bulb that hung by a cord from the ceiling.

I was only nine, but I knew which house I wanted. There was no comparison between the two. I wanted the Craftsman, old though it was, because it simply oozed charm, class, and atmosphere. It was inconvenient with only one bathroom, no central heating, and single-pane windows, which were not very energy efficient. It was a home designed for a previous era. Fortunately, it was also the one Mom and Dad decided to buy. I was elated!

Yes, the upper story was unheated, but who cares about little things like central heating when you are nine? For the first time ever, I was in love with a house. The reality was that in the winter we didn't spend much time upstairs. It was too cold! Mom gave us hot-water bottles to take to bed at night. We also had several blankets piled high on each of our beds. The one bathroom for seven people was the larger problem, but that didn't register as that big of an issue back then. I could still remember when Grandma and Grandpa first got indoor plumbing, so one bathroom seemed perfectly adequate to us. I think two bathrooms might have even seemed a bit uppity.

Oh, Jeff, this house had so many architectural virtues—that beautiful staircase, just to name one! When I was in high school, my prom dates would nervously sit in the front room waiting for me to come down the stairs. Clad in my prom dress, I carefully placed each high-heeled foot on a stair. I wore a tiara on my head, which I kept regally still, inclined slightly toward my date as I slowly and precariously descended. In those moments, I felt like a movie star.

Mom and Dad remodeled the house after I moved out, and I regretted every change they made to the structure of this beautiful home. They made it warmer in the winter by lowering the ceilings and adding central heat. And they took some space from the den to put in an extra bathroom, which was very useful, but took away some of the original character.

They also replaced the original kitchen cabinets with modern cabinets, and they removed the French doors to open up the floor plan for family living. It was all understandable, but I just didn't like it. That old house lost much of its charm when they updated its original architecture. For years, I dreamed of your dad and I buying it and restoring it to its original glory. But we were never going to live in our hometown. We'd moved on.

Well, that was certainly a walk down memory lane, wasn't it, Jeff? I'm going to try not to think about losing the family home and instead focus on some of the new and wonderful memories that your dad and I have created for you kids at our ranch house west of Boise. We've had some great times there over the past 20 years. Your dad and I still love our home, but nobody uses the pool anymore. Your sisters aren't living here, and they don't ride enough to make it practical to have horses taking up space in the pasture. And while I enjoyed all the gardening over the years, it's getting to be a bit more work than I want to tackle each spring and fall.

Your dad is loath to move, but I'd like to be closer to town, work, and the golf course. Yes, I've been bitten by the golf bug, Jeff. I seem to be a bit obsessed with flailing away at a little white ball that sits absolutely still, trying to hit it smartly down the fairway. Sounds easy, doesn't it? Well, it's remarkably difficult to hit it cleanly and make it fly high and straight. And for some reason, I'm very happy to spend 4 or more hours trying to do just that, over and over for 18 holes.

I'd better stop writing now, Jeff. I have laundry, housework, yard work, and all my usual chores to get started on. Since I'm working during the week, I can't afford to waste my weekends, and I need to get most of my work done today. I'm planning to go to church tomorrow morning, and maybe your dad and I will fit in a golf game in the afternoon.

Stay well and we'll see you soon. And please, try and have some fun. Play with the animals, tell your jokes, let the church ladies spoil you on Sunday. Before you know it, you'll be on the plane, heading home to spend the 4th of July with us in Idaho, where we'll all be waiting for you. And remember, we all love you very much.

Letter 13

Kaber Health Care

Well, Jeff, I am feeling the need to sit down and write you another long letter. First of all, we were so upset to hear that you came down with pneumonia. You know that your dad and I wanted to get down there to be with you. In fact, we were getting ready to call the airline to arrange a trip when we got your call from the hospital. You calmed us with your wry comment, "You don't need to come all the way down here. I won't croak." And indeed you did not. Shortly thereafter you were back at Kaber, resting in your room with your beloved staff members, Lena and Karen, who were fussing over you.

I marvel over the number of kind, dedicated, and competent people who have cared for you, traveled to Idaho with you, and become part of our family for a period of time. Of course they come into our lives only to leave after a few months or more.

We feel sad whenever they leave and wonder if you will ever have anyone so caring and kind in your life at Kaber again. And then the staff regroups, shakes itself, and, like magic, another one surfaces.

Your dad and I, however, are become increasingly worried about your health. We were told at the beginning of this saga that you would improve with therapy for a period of time and then plateau. What we didn't really understand, or maybe chose to ignore, is that you would also slide down the other side at some point. During our recent visits to Texas, and your visits to see us in Idaho, we noticed that you were having more trouble holding yourself upright and walking. As time went on, we saw that you were relying on your wheelchair more and more.

We spoke to your case manager at Kaber about your recent bout with pneumonia, and he said that you were probably aspirating your food, which may have caused it. I was relieved to hear that they are arranging for an occupational therapist to come to Kaber and work with you on your swallowing. We are hoping that you will try your hardest, Jeff. This is very important. You need to retain your walking, talking, and swallowing skills, which you worked so hard to regain.

Since your last visit home, many things have changed around here. Your sister Amy graduated from college with an engineering degree and accepted a job in Phoenix. She will be moving in August, which should give her a realistic idea of the worst weather Phoenix has to offer. And Pam is considering going back to college. She's thinking of maybe majoring in business, with an emphasis on computers. She finds the cosmetology business a bit draining. It's amazing, all the troubles people confide in her while sitting in her chair. The problem is she can't leave their issues at work. Instead, she packs them up and takes them home with her.

Pam and little Taylor, who is five years old now, had some excitement in their lives not long ago. They were driving home one cold, winter night, when Pam noticed a red cast to the sky just a block away from their home. She was curious, so she drove down the street to see what was causing this phenomenon. As she turned the corner, she could see that a house was on fire, but she didn't see any fire trucks. As your sister reached for her cell phone to call the fire department, she saw a young woman running down the street wearing nothing but her panic.

Pam later learned that this poor woman had been in the shower when the fire started. It spread so rapidly that she had to leave her house without even having a chance to grab a towel. The woman apparently ran through the fire and out the front door, going from house to house, banging on the doors for help. Nobody answered. Then Pam came along. It was obvious to her that something was very wrong, so she stopped the car to see if she could help. She opened the car door, and the young woman more or less fell in. Pam took her home, and the woman collapsed down on the carpet.

Pam called 911 and was told to immediately put her in a tepid shower until the ambulance arrived. The woman was hospitalized and later sent by air ambulance to the burn center in Salt Lake City. Last I heard, she was on the road to recovery. And your sister was written up in the newspaper as an example of a Good Samaritan. That's our girl. She has a big heart, and she thinks fast in an emergency.

I told you over the phone, Jeff, that your grandmother died back in December. She fought the good fight against a horrible disease. They told her that 5 years was the average life span with multiple myeloma; she survived for 13—and except for this past year, was able to care for her garden and take the occasional trip with your grandpa. I am thankful that we were able to take a cruise to Hawaii and Tahiti with my parents last winter. The doctor allowed your grandmother to go off the chemo for the trip so she would feel as good as possible.

I tried to store up memories of her during this trip. I remember one day when Mom and I were standing on the rock-solid remains of a volcano and we noticed a small green plant forcing its way through the lava. As we stood together looking at that resilient little plant, I imprinted that moment into my memory. Mom was like that little plant. She didn't give up: She fought her disease with dignity and determination.

We all went with Mom and Dad to her last doctor's appointment. We were quite a crowd—Linda, Laureen, me, and Mom and Dad. When the doctor entered the examination room, he took one startled look at us all sitting there, turned on his heel, and went to fetch his nurse.

He must have thought we were going to gang up on him about something. Actually, your grandmother asked us to come along. She had trouble remembering anything the doctor said at this point. After the examination, the doctor told us, "Your mother is dying, and she is dying fast." He said her kidneys were failing and that it would be a swift and kind death for someone in this condition.

It wasn't a surprise to hear that the end was near, since she had been losing ground quickly the last month or so. Even though we were somewhat prepared, this was still tough news for all of us to process. After that appointment, we contacted hospice care and Father Riffle. Hospice came by for the initial evaluation, and Father Riffle came to the house to perform the last rites. Mom was comforted by this final sacrament, a fact that surprised her. She said that she thought it would be scary, but that it was nice.

I then got into my "stay busy, don't let your feelings overcome you" mode. I decided that the Christmas tree had to go up. After all, it was December, and I wanted Mom to be able to enjoy it, even though she might not be with us by Christmas. So I dragged it out, placed it in the living room, and my sisters and I decorated it. We turned the Christmas tree lights on, and it did dissipate our gloom somewhat. Late that afternoon, your grandmother sat by her living room windows, looking out at the snow. I brought her a cup of coffee, which she sipped and held to warm her hands. Linda and I decided that we should stay the night, in case she or my dad needed us. Laureen had to go home to her family.

When I woke up the next morning, I went into Mom's bedroom. She was unresponsive. I went and got Linda and then called your dad. Linda, Laureen, and I were by her side throughout that morning. My dad was there, too, but he couldn't seem to stay in her room. He would come in, then dart right back out again, trotting back and forth to the neighbor's house.

I could tell he was too upset to stay. I wasn't feeling very strong either. I basically hid my face in the bed covers, holding onto my mom's arm until she passed. She died peacefully. Soon after, your dad arrived. He held me close as I cried. He took care of notifying the coroner and calling Father Riffle, who came by to offer us some comfort. The people that came to pick up Mom advised us to step outside before she was zipped into a bag and taken away. They told us, "You don't want this to be your last memory." So we waited outside in the cold until she was gone.

I miss her so much, Jeff. When I'm in the garden, working, I often head for the phone to call her with a question or comment about a plant. We shared a deep love for gardening and spent hours together wandering through our respective gardens, discussing the performance of our plants, especially roses and irises. I wonder how much time will go by before I no longer turn and grab the phone to call my mother.

When we are together, Jeff, I rarely share any of my life with you. Those conversations don't seem to go anywhere. You have a limited capacity to grasp anything outside of your small orbit, so I write you letters instead. Writing these letters with you in mind makes me feel as though I am reaching right through the ravages of the head injury, straight through to my son.

Right now, I want to tell you about the job I got a few years ago. I'm still amazed at how a small-town girl from Moscow was suddenly offered a job by the governor of Idaho, especially a girl who had delayed graduating from college until she was 39. Anyway, one of my friends that I met through my job is married to our governor's chief of staff. A position opened up that needed to be filled quickly.

Basically, my friend's husband came home from work one day complaining about this problem he was expected to solve. And my friend recommended me to be the bureau chief of our state licensing bureau! Can you believe it? Her husband, Mike, called me and asked if I was interested in coming in for an interview for the position that had just opened up. Your dad and I discussed it at length. He was a bit worried about my accepting a job at that level, since I had only been working professionally for seven years. I told your dad that I at least wanted to go and meet with Mike.

So, Mike and I arranged a time for the interview. I was nervous, but our conversation seemed to go okay. After we spoke, Mike said he wanted to introduce me to the governor. We walked right into the governor's office, sat down, and the three of us had a conversation. As Mike and I were leaving the office, the governor told Mike to have me sign the papers for the job.

Mike said he had planned on having me think about it for a week, and then we would get together again when I had made my decision. But the governor turned to me and asked me if I wanted the job. I was able to croak out a yes, and Mike was told to sign me up!

I left the governor's office in somewhat of a daze. I walked down the hall, drumming my fists into my thighs and mumbling, "Oh no, oh no, what have I done?" Well, Jeff, you know how I like to arrange things, carefully organizing gardens, quilts, and closets. Your dad might also say husbands. Just about anything that doesn't involve paper is pretty much in my purview.

It turned out that organization was what was needed in my new position. And I wasn't on my own. My former bosses at the legislative auditor's office helped me with every aspect of the changes I made, and within a year or so, everything seemed to be running pretty smoothly. My first big decision was whether to fire a couple of employees that had come under scrutiny a few months before I joined as bureau chief. I decided to keep both of them—a decision that I came to question years later. Both of these employees eventually left the bureau, but under much more difficult circumstances than if I had made that decision in the beginning.

Then, the biggest calamity struck: Our health insurance was canceled by the insurance company! We had been experiencing problems with the insurance company for years, as the premiums were increasing annually. Finally, the premiums became so high that they were just about equal to the amount of money we received monthly from the original insurance settlement for your accident. When we didn't drop out, which we were sure was the insurance company's intent with the sky-high premiums, they canceled our policy!

We don't have close to the income needed to support you at Kaber, or any other place that can handle your care, Jeff. After careful consideration, your dad and I decided our only option was to file suit against the insurance company. Your dad did some research, and eventually we settled upon some attorneys in San Francisco, who were supplemented by an attorney here in Boise.

I don't think I can adequately explain the stress of what it's like to sue a major insurance company. It's like going up against Hercules with a sling shot. We have been throwing all our resources into this fight. Your dad's law practice has been dwindling because much of his time is spent helping out the attorneys: going over documents, providing documentation, answering questions, and always being on call at a moment's notice.

For my part, I am not as strong emotionally as I was before your accident. Even so, I have been able to cope with everything that has been thrown at me so far. I was able to remain strong while you were in the hospital, and I tried to be your coach while you were at the Elks, undergoing rehabilitation. Looking back, I also managed to mostly hold it together while you were at home with us, and throughout the moves between different facilities in Texas. But I think, between the lawsuit and personnel issues at work, I may have reached my limit. I feel more fragile emotionally and physically. I seriously wonder if I can cope any longer. And I know your dad is worried about me, along with his own stress from dealing with all the legal matters.

During this time, I attended a national convention at the request of one of our boards at the bureau. The convention was in Tucson, Arizona, and I fell in love with the desert! Something about the area really calmed my soul. There was a cactus garden at the resort, so I would just sit outside on a bench or stroll along the paths, among the cacti and other desert plants. I found that a feeling of calm was settling over me, helping me relax my muscles and unclench my jaw. I called your dad and told him how much I loved being in Tucson. He joined me a couple of days later. He likes to tell people that I told him to bring his checkbook, which is just his little joke. In any event, we both enjoyed our short escape into the peace of the desert. It seemed like an oasis for our nerves, which were jangled from the continuous stress we'd been living with for too long.

I've heard that small miracles occur in our lives that we don't even recognize as miracles when they're happening. You are well aware, Jeff, that your dad is not an impulsive man. He likes to save dollars rather than spend them. So, it seems totally out of the realm of possibility that your dad would suddenly decide to buy a house in Arizona, but six months later, that is exactly what he did. And not content with just buying a house, he also decided we should join a country club with an incredible golf course!

We never thought of ourselves as country-club people, Jeff. We'd never even discussed joining one before this trip to Arizona. The answer to this riddle is that I have this incredible man at my side—who buys a house and joins a country club—because he is doing his best to take care of his wife during some very difficult circumstances. Well, it turned out to be a wonderful decision for the both of us.

We have been escaping down there whenever possible, and I believe that this oasis of calm in Tucson has saved my sanity. We golf almost every day while we are there, and the course is amazing. I attend Mass on Sunday in a beautiful church in our neighborhood. And behind the altar is a clear window with a view of the mountains. So, all I have to do is sit there in the serenity of that church and look out the window, and my soul finds peace.

While I find faith and golfing peaceful, the habits I have developed over time to help cope with stress are difficult to change. Even though trips to Tucson were helping us catch our breath and recoup, I was noticing that I was no longer happy when we'd return to Boise. I was no longer enjoying my job, so I tried to fix that by adding more work to my already-full schedule.

I went to a national convention of the architect boards. As usual, your dad joined me later in the week. At the convention, I was offered a position on one of the national committees, which is an honor granted to only a few state administrators. I was considering accepting the new role, but your dad was not happy about it. He felt that I was already stretched to the max and that this would only add to my increased stress levels. He said, "I know you. You won't just do what is required." He was so puzzled with me, adding, "Why are you even considering accepting this appointment?"

I wanted to consider what your father was saying, so I thought about it some more overnight. I am not particularly introspective, so I hadn't spent much time analyzing why I tended to fill every day of my life with so much activity. But reflecting on this tendency, with your father's prodding, I came to the conclusion that I was trying to find something—anything—that would distract me from the stressful world I was then inhabiting. Your dad and I had a long talk. We decided that I would resign my job with the bureau.

When we got home after the convention, I organized my files, tied up any loose ends, and then wrote my letter of resignation to the governor. I knew it was the right decision, although I had some regrets. I had worked for three governors over the past seven years, and our relationships had been positive. I had enjoyed working with the various boards and learning about their professions. I had presented both rule and law changes to the legislature. In short, I was walking away from a job where I felt like I had made significant contributions. With all that said, it was time for me to go.

I love sharing my thoughts, concerns, and life with you in these letters, Jeff. I so wish you could have grown up, chosen your own life path, and pursued your dreams, instead of all that you are experiencing now. We could be sitting down together, maybe having a glass of wine before dinner as we let each other into our respective worlds. Or maybe we would just sit together and quietly enjoy each other's company. But this is our reality, and I do feel closer to you through these writings. I'm afraid I need to stop for now, though. The mundane chores of the day are tugging at me, and I need to get dinner ready for your dad and me.

Goodbye for now, my son. I'll write again soon.

Letter 14

Kaber Health Care

Hi, Jeff. You've been on my mind a lot lately. I want to sit down, collect my thoughts, and write to you again, but there doesn't seem to be any good way to start this letter. I always try to find something that connects us in a positive manner, when I string words together on these pages. Unfortunately, my thoughts and concerns right now begin and end with your seriously failing health and your inability to walk—or even stand. I think I am just too caught up in this to think happy thoughts right now.

There have been so many hospitalizations, starting with your bouts of pneumonia, which began a couple of years ago. And now you can no longer help yourself when you need to get around from your chair to the bed, or into the shower, or even the toilet. The staff members tell us that you are now dead weight, requiring total care. It seems too soon for you to lose the skills you gained during all those years of therapy. I just don't want to believe that this is even happening. It took so long for you to learn how to swallow, talk, stand, and then walk. And now, the slide back down seems to be happening so fast that we are all struggling to process this. How can any of us be positive with this new and unkind reality in the forefront of our thoughts and emotions?

In spite of this, I guess I should take a moment and count our blessings. We are very fortunate that we have the resources to take care of you, Jeff. I need to focus on some of the positives in our situation. It was such a relief when our lawsuit with the insurance company settled; that is one huge problem off our shoulders. It seems like when one big issue disappears, however, another one emerges to take its place. And your declining health is a hard one to accept.

At least you had some fun when you traveled to Phoenix for your birthday. I take comfort in that and am glad that your doctor felt it was safe for you to visit with your sister for a short time. Amy wanted it to be a special time for you. She told me that she'd decorated the house with a "Happy 40th Birthday, Jeff" poster and black crepe paper streamers, to set the proper mood! Amy said many of her friends came over to help you celebrate. She was concerned, though. She said you were barely awake much of the time you were in Phoenix. I hope you were awake long enough to have some fun at your party, though.

When Christmas rolled around, we were anxious to see for ourselves how you were doing. We were hoping that you would be in better health than Amy reported in September. During that visit, however, we also became more and more worried about your lethargy. You were barely able to join in with the family, because you basically nodded off in your wheelchair, once you were up for the day. After you returned to Kaber, we spoke to your doctor about our observations. He said he would cut back on any medications that could be causing the lethargy. We all hoped that would help some, Jeff. We were all worried about you.

Do you remember that in the spring, Amy and I made a trip to see you? This was just before your dad and I left Tucson for Boise. I flew to Phoenix, and your sister and I boarded a plane for Austin. As usual, we all stayed at the La Quinta closest to Kaber. (You like to have a vacation from Kaber, and you really look forward to the pancakes the hotel serves in the morning. You are always content with the hotel coffee, but Amy and I are persnickety, I guess. We actually made an emergency trip to Starbucks before we joined you for breakfast.)

Later in the day, after your accompanying staff members had carefully maneuvered you into the shower and cleaned you up, we all trooped out to the pool area. We made quite a procession, Jeff: you in your wheelchair, two staff members, Amy, and me. You loved spending time in the spa. In the past, you were able to step down into the spa with a staff member holding on to your hands, helping you to balance. This time, however, two staff members had to lower you down into the warm, bubbly water. You must have enjoyed it, because you stayed in the hot tub until you resembled a soggy prune. We took several pictures on that trip. My favorite is of you and Amy by the spa. You both looked so happy—Amy with her head bent to your level, her long strawberry-blonde hair falling down between you.

Eventually you needed to be helped out of the hot tub, which was much more difficult then helping you in. Now that you are basically dead weight, both staff members had to get into the spa and carefully lift your slippery body up and into the wheel-chair—while trying not to slip, themselves. I stood nervously by, not strong enough to be helpful. The staffers were strong and experienced, so you were safely transferred from the water to your wheelchair. This was a good visit, but, sadly, we noticed that your physical condition had declined.

And then in May, we got a call telling us that you were back in the hospital. This wasn't the usual pneumonia, but a block-age of your intestinal tract. This hospitalization came on so sud-denly, and your condition was so serious, that I think it just caught everyone off guard. But what really bothered me was that no one seemed to know why the blockage happened. At least when you had pneumonia, as serious as that can be, we had some idea of the cause.

Due to the seriousness of your condition with the intestinal blockage, your dad and I planned to take an emergency trip to Austin. Soon after, however, we got a phone call from Kaber, tell-ing us that you were much better and would soon be discharged from the hospital. So, we canceled our emergency trip, and I began planning to visit you in June with Pam and Taylor.

It was so good to see that big smile on your face when you arrived at the hotel and saw your sister and niece standing there with me. We were surprised to find you almost back to your old self. Your spirits were good and your overall energy level was much improved. After your last visit to the hospital with such a serious condition, we expected to find you in worse shape than you were at Christmas. Instead, your condition seemed much improved, which was such a welcome surprise!

One of my favorite memories of this trip is when all of us

were in our hotel room, eating pizza for dinner. After we ate, you asked Taylor to sing you a song. She sat on your lap and sang the Dixie Chicks' "Travelin' Soldier" over and over for you. Taylor has a beautiful voice, but is often reluctant to perform. She made an exception for you, though.

Taylor has been such a joy for your dad and me. She was so easy to have around from the moment she arrived on this earth. Your dad and I have had her with us just about every weekend for these past 12 years. As an only child, she has always been comfortable around adults—maybe too comfortable, because it's easy to forget she's just a kid. In fact, a year or so ago, Taylor and I were hanging around in the kitchen. I was busy throwing dinner together when she made some offhanded remark that struck me the wrong way. Without thinking, I said, "Why are you behaving like such a child?" My jaw dropped when I realized what I had just said. I mean, Taylor's still only 12, even though she often seems to be going on 22. I guess she *should* be childish for a few more years, like every other kid her age.

I don't remember if we told you, but Pam is now a college graduate. She went back to college a few years ago and proved to herself what we have always known: She is very smart. Even very smart people have to open a textbook now and again, though, to get good grades. A technicality I think Pam may have ignored the first time around.

Pam became determined to finish college after she brought a guy she was seriously dating to one of our family reunions. At that time, she was working, but apparently she wasn't all that fulfilled with her job. She'd been talking about going back to college but hadn't done anything about it yet. Anyway, at the reunion, she introduced this guy to Amy and her girl cousins—a group that included a physician, a professor, and an engineer. Pam came home feeling annoyed at herself for what she considered her lack of accomplishment and decided to make some changes.

She enrolled in college shortly thereafter, majoring in computer information systems. During her second semester back in school, she was awarded a $1,000 grant for a single parent who was studying business. And during her third and fourth semester, she made the dean's list. She was taking all upper-division classes. And now she has her college degree and a job in her field! We are so proud of her—but also puzzled, as all parents probably are when some haphazard event turns your kid around after you've spent years trying to inspire them. If you need a visual, just picture me pulling my hair out by the handful.

After telling you this story about Pam, I might as well tell you how Amy ended up majoring in engineering. You might think it was due to our thoughtful evaluation of her strengths, and then our encouragement, that brought all this about. In fact, your dad and I had tried to steer her in that direction from the beginning, but she decided to major in international business and French. Now, picture her in the first quarter of her senior year of college. She has a chance conversation with her boyfriend about their SAT scores. When he heard what her score was in math, which was higher than his, he scoffed, "Well, why aren't you majoring in engineering, then?"

She gave this some thought and, shortly thereafter, marched herself into the Department of Engineering and told them she wanted to change her major. A degree in engineering requires some very specific courses. It took Amy three more years to complete her education. Again, I am very proud of her, but it's a wonder I'm not bald from pulling out my hair!

I'm sorry you never had the chance to go to college, Jeff. I had wanted it so much for you, too. It seems so unfair that you are lying in a hospital bed, unable to move freely around your room. We kept hoping, for years, that things would look up for you. We hoped you would be able to move about with ease. We hoped your vision could be improved. We hoped you would be able to control your emotions. We hoped you could finish high school and attend college. And we hoped you could someday live independently. It seemed as though all our hopes just died, one after another, as the years went by. And as bad as we feel, we know how much more difficult this situation has been for you.

I think I will just close this letter now. I am going to try and remember the nice visit we had with you in June and hope that your health continues to improve. We all love you, Jeff.

Letter 15

Boise Home, Idaho

Dear Jeff,

Your dad and I received a call from Kaber on the 16th of August, informing us that you were in the hospital again. Apparently, you complained of stomach pain and, with your history of the intestinal blockage last spring, the folks at Kaber took you right to the hospital. I called and spoke to the staff, and it seemed like everything was being handled appropriately. Nothing we discussed set off any internal alarms. We were concerned, of course. We were always concerned with your hospitalizations. You've been hospitalized so many times that I guess we've become a bit desensitized. We expected a call in a couple of days, telling us that you were back at Kaber.

Unfortunately, that was not to be. At 4:15 in the morning on

August 19th, the phone by our bedside started ringing. I jerked awake, turned over, and clawed around in the dark for the receiver. No good news comes at that hour, and when I finally grabbed the receiver, my heart was pounding. It was Ron Marsh, the case manager from Kaber Health Services, informing us that you had taken a turn for the worse, adding that "it didn't look good." Ron said the hospital staff had placed you on a ventilator, and the doctor in charge wanted us to immediately call him at the hospital. We were in Idaho, you were in Texas. Two thousand miles separated us from you, the hospital, and those with any information about your condition.

Your dad and I spent the next two hours in a state of increasing frustration. We called the number that Ron gave us right away, and then spent considerable time explaining, to whomever answered, that we were told to call that number. It was excruciating, Jeff. Ron said there was some urgency in the matter. A doctor was supposed to be at the other end, anxious to speak with us! Instead, we were routed to at least three other numbers, with the same exasperating result. Time kept passing, and we were becoming frantic!

At last, we received a call from what sounded like a very young doctor. We were both on the line and feeling pretty desperate to get information about you. We had lots of questions, but either she could not or would not answer them. Eventually, a pulmonary specialist came to the phone, and he gave us a great deal of information, more than our frantic, sleep-deprived brains could fully absorb.

I am sure the pulmonary specialist believed he was using very simple language, but it's difficult for the layperson to understand technical information, especially while in a state of shock. That being said, what I heard was that you were having multiple system failures. The doctor said you had awoken during the night, unable to breathe adequately. That is why you were on a ventilator.

He said you had been vomiting—which no drugs had been able to control, not even the strongest drugs, used for chemotherapy patients—and that you had been aspirating the vomit. He said that they had run a tube up through your nose to your lungs, to try and clear them, and that your gut was distended, because you had developed another intestinal blockage.

The doctor said you would no longer be able to process food through your gut, that you would always need a feeding tube. He also said you would need a tracheotomy, just so you could breathe. And with all this, they were unable to relieve your pain with medication, because of your falling blood pressure.

As we received this news, we were growing increasingly worried. It sounded like you were dying. We were both in shock, wondering how could this be happening. I wanted to cry in frustration, to rush out there so we could be with you. Instead, I turned to your dad, hoping somehow he could make some sense out of all this. But the bad news just kept coming.

The doctor then stressed that the "hard decision" had to be made and made quickly. We could hardly absorb the situation. I didn't know what the right decision was. My mind was still trying to cope with what was happening to you. It sounded like the doctor was telling us that you were dying, and that you were in horrible pain from the blockage, and even worse pain from the respirator. Desperate for any information that would help us, I asked the doctor what he would do if it were his loved one. He said he would give his loved one "comfort medicine." I asked him what that meant. He said you would be given medication to calm you and relieve your pain. They would then be able to remove the respirator.

Oh, Jeff. I didn't know what to do! I was frantic that you were in so much unrelenting pain. The doctor told us that having a respirator without sedation was the worst thing that could happen to someone. And the doctor gave us no hope that you would improve. You were dying and in horrible pain and discomfort. After talking it over with your dad, we made the hard decision to give you comfort medicine and to remove the respirator. We knew there was a risk because of your low blood pressure, but try as we might, we couldn't find a better alternative.

Your dad then made the arrangements for our emergency trip to Austin. The earliest we could catch a flight was 2:30 p.m. We scrambled around to prepare for that trip, hoping we could reach your bedside in time. And I still held out some small hope that you would recover. You had bounced back from serious conditions before; maybe you could do it again.

But we were never to board that plane, Jeff. We would not be able to sit by your side in the hospital, hold your hand, talk to the doctors in person, or discuss possible treatments. About an hour and a half after our phone conversation with the doctor, we received a call from Ron telling us that you were gone.

I had rehearsed this moment in my mind many times. Ever since your accident, I knew I would receive that call someday. I always imagined I'd be by your side for the days or weeks that remained of our time together on earth. We would have time to talk, or just quietly sit together, and I would have time to summon a priest for the final sacraments. I'd also have time to absorb what was happening, maybe even to get some closure as

I came to terms with the fact that I would not see you again in this lifetime.

I remember one of your bouts of pneumonia that was pretty serious. We thought we might lose you then. Your life had turned out to be so hard, with too many health challenges and physical problems to overcome or endure. I then had the thought that maybe it would be better for you to finally have peace. And then my thoughts screamed *no*. That would not be better. I couldn't imagine living in a world where you were not also drawing breath, not available to touch or hold.

And now, that was our reality. And despite having walked through this scene in my mind, I was totally unprepared. My heart felt heavy with pain, and my mind wouldn't be still so I could think. I looked to your dad to get me through that day. He held me up with his strength and his ability to think logically when the world seems upside down. And he was there when we needed to make more hard decisions in the days to come.

A few days later, after I got over the first shock, I became obsessed with getting more information. I needed to learn more about your final days. I called Kaber in hopes of speaking to Lena and Karen, who had been with you during your last two days. Karen told us that on the 18th of August, she answered a phone call midday. She said the voice on the other end asked clearly if Lena was there. Karen said "yes" and asked who was calling. She was very surprised when the caller clearly identified himself as Jeff. Your familiar voice, Jeff, the voice she heard every day, could barely be understood. She said this voice was very different—that this voice spoke with clarity. Puzzled, she told you that she would get Lena.

Lena told me, in our conversation, that she came to the phone and asked you how you were doing. "Not very well" was your response. You asked her if she would be your staff member at the hospital the next day. Lena said she would. Later that day, at the normal assignment meeting, Lena thought about being silent when volunteers were requested to staff you the following day. But, remembering her conversation with you, she volunteered and was selected.

Lena also told me how much she loved you, Jeff, and how much you had given to her. She said you told her every day how beautiful she was. Lena once said to you, "Jeff, you are blind. How do you know I am beautiful?" You told her, "I don't need to see to know you are beautiful." Sobbing, she told me that she had nobody else to tell her she was beautiful.

Amy called Mike, a former staff member who had been very close to you and our family, to tell him of your death. He told her how you had impacted his life. Apparently he was prone to depression. He said his depression gradually left him during the time he worked with you at Kaber. He credits you with helping to change his condition, by the courage and humor you showed in facing life with all of your disabilities head-on.

Both Lena and Ron had been by your side when you quietly ceased to breathe. Lena told me that when they gave you comfort medicine, the tension gradually left your body. You continued to hold her hand as the stress and agony left your face and your muscles relaxed. And then, at some point, you were finally at peace—26 years after the accident that had ended your young life as you knew it, leaving you with a broken body and a broken mind. The accident completely changed who you were, but head injuries can do that. The Jeff we knew before the accident was one person, and the Jeff we came to know after the accident was another. And I want you to know that we loved both of you.

At home, we began the painful process of arranging for your funeral. We were not of an age to begin thinking of our final resting place, so we had no cemetery in mind for us, much less our eldest child. This whole situation was way out of whack! Parents should not have to bury their children. Neither time, nor the comfort of a priest, nor the sympathy and support of friends and family can buffer you from the shock and pain you feel when you arrange for the final disposition of your child.

Larry and I were guided through the whole process by the funeral director. He was very kind and patient as we chose the verses, the service memorials, and your headstone. And then we had to arrange the church service. Father Riffle had retired, and Father Henry was the new pastor at our church. Yet, I wanted Father Riffle to perform the funeral. He had been our family priest since we started attending church regularly 23 years ago. But for that, we needed Father Henry's permission. Father Henry was so kind and understanding. He said, "Of course you want your family priest to perform the service," and graciously stepped aside.

The night before the funeral, we held a rosary service. Three people from Kaber flew to Boise for both the rosary and your funeral. It was right for them to be there. They had been your family in Texas, all these years. Lena and Karen cared lovingly for you and were with you on the last days of your life. Lena had been by your side when life left your body. David, the manager of Kaber, spoke at the rosary. He described how you had impacted their lives by how you courageously faced life with all of your difficulties.

I invited them to our house after the service. They declined the offer, and I could feel that a separation had already occurred. They were no longer linked with our family in the same way they had been before your passing. There would be no more holiday trips to Boise for them. And there would be no more trips to Austin for us. They would no longer be a part of our lives. And I'm sure they, too, were emotionally exhausted—with their love for you, Jeff, and the pain of this loss. They, too, had families to care for, and they needed to reserve themselves for their own lives. But I still grieved for the loss of this link to you, tenuous as it was.

Your family, and many of our friends, attended your funeral. The folks from Kaber were there, and, as I suspected, that was the last we ever saw of them. It was such a comfort to have Father Riffle conducting your service. When we were planning your funeral, he said that he pictured you now walking with Jesus, his arm around your shoulders. I held on to that picture. In the church, there were candles on each side of the altar, and their flames flickered throughout the Mass. I fancied that your spirit was joining us, flying through the air, causing the candle flames to dance with joy in celebration of your new freedom of movement.

That October, your dad and I celebrated 40 years of marriage. Your sisters had been busy for months arranging a party for us. Our relatives and friends were all invited. With everybody already planning to travel to Boise, your dad and I decided that was when we would hold your memorial. We set it for the day before our anniversary. Amy put together a DVD of your life, with photos and carefully chosen music. I received a copy a couple of weeks before the event. I must have watched that DVD 10 times, trying to go through it often enough so I would not cry during the actual service. That never happened, though; I cried every single time I watched it. I finally decided that a mother had a right to bawl all the way through her son's memorial. It turned out okay, though. Everybody else joined me in shedding ample tears.

Your ashes were placed in an urn, and you were buried in Dry Creek Cemetery. It is the closest well-tended cemetery to our home in the country, which you loved so much. We found a headstone with a carving of a home that looks very much like ours. We even purchased a plot next to yours, for the future. Soon after, Amy called us and said, "I want one, too. I don't want to be alone." So, we ended up buying enough plots for all of our little family, just in case they want to be there, too. We hope to be long gone before any of them have to make that decision, though.

I have been reflecting on our lives since your accident, Jeff, trying to make some sense of it all. I know I have changed. I don't feel like I have control over events in my life anymore. Of course, I never did, but I didn't know that until my world fell apart one morning while I was digging weeds out of my garden. None of us deserved what happened that day. We were not evil people. We tried to go through life without unduly disturbing the environment or causing harm to others. We made an effort to help our friends and family, and even strangers, whenever we saw a need.

I feel very fortunate that I never felt angry with God. Instead, I leaned on Him in the days, months, and years to follow. I didn't allow myself to feel hatred toward the negligent farmer, who I believe didn't do enough to keep you or the other workers safe. I instinctively knew that I didn't have room to fight for

159

you and hate him at the same time. So, of course, I chose you. I remember saying to God, "This man will have to die and face you someday. You will deal with this and pass out punishment, or not, as you see fit." Then, I was able to mostly let it go. Oh, I had the occasional flare-up of anger, but it passed eventually. I had enough to deal with. I simply couldn't carry around that burden, too.

I remember reading in the paper about this farmer's death years later. At the time, I felt a sense of relief. At that point, I knew the issue had been put to rest. I believe he faced his maker, and the scales were balanced, whatever the judgment was. It wasn't mine to determine, and I never wished for any outcome, one way or another.

But how did your life make sense, Jeff? That was what troubled me. Sometimes it kept me up at night, as I tried to make sense of it all. You once said to me, several years after your accident, that you thought you knew why it happened. You said that you believed you would have gotten involved with drugs. I listened, but I didn't challenge your statement or agree with it. I just held your hand as we sat with that idea.

Later, I reflected on your acceptance of what happened and why it happened. Your reasoning is an example of a "greater good." As I understand this principle, when a horrible tragedy occurs, maybe totally undeserved, there may be a greater good that will somehow come out of it. The biblical story of Joseph, who was sold into slavery by his brothers, is a good example of this principle.

Joseph was sold to merchants by his jealous brothers, and then ended up in Egypt, where he found favor and was eventually made governor over Egypt. He foresaw, in a dream, seven years of plenty, followed by seven years of famine. During the years of plenty, he stored up food for Egypt for the years of famine. Eventually, his brothers came to Egypt to buy grain during the famine. Joseph recognized them and had them gather their father and their animals and move to Egypt, so they would not starve. The brothers said, "Here we are before you as your slaves." But Joseph said to them, "Don't be afraid; I can't put myself in the place of God. You plotted evil against me, but God turned it into good, in order to preserve the lives of many people who are alive today because of what happened."[1]

Jeff, like Joseph, you believed that your life was serving a greater good. You believed that your accident saved you from a worse fate, involvement with drugs. Your accident had an impact on our whole family. I can't say how it affected or changed your sisters or your dad. I can only speak for myself.

Before your accident, I charged through life, imagining that through my determination and careful planning, life would go on being pleasant and rewarding. We worked hard and were prudent with money. I exercised regularly and watched my diet. We provided for our children and exposed them to religion, music, sports, and a decent education. I felt in control and imagined that we were living the American dream.

And then the nightmare began, and I put all my efforts into changing your reality. A doctor once told me that he could feel the force of determination coming off of me. He was worried about me and wanted to prescribe some medication for anxiety. I declined—I thought I was doing okay. A few years later, he

---

1   Gen. 50:18–20. *Good News Bible.* Bible Societies/HarperCollins Publishers Ltd UK, 1992.

turned out to be right. I was falling apart. And that is when I gave in and quit imagining that I could control my little part of the world. I needed to back off, settle down, reflect, and find some peace.

My peace came through my faith, my church, and the continuing love and support of my family. I first decided to find out what this church of my childhood was all about. Of course, I had taken catechism classes in grade school, but that was long ago. And those classes were aimed at children. I needed to be catechized on an adult level.

First, I read our entire adult catechism, front to back. That's a big book! Then I started listening to EWTN, a Catholic radio station started by a scrappy little nun known as Mother Angelica. I mainly listened to a program called *Catholic Answers Live*, which features live callers with questions about the Church, their faith, and everything in between. Those questions, and the answers, really helped with my understanding of the Church, the Bible, and my spiritual journey.

I also attended several retreats. And I read, lots and lots of books, including the Bible, mainly the New Testament. Throughout this process, I started changing. I learned to sit in the quiet. I learned to reflect. I learned to enjoy being alone. Eventually, I found an abiding faith and peace. Without your accident, I imagine that I would have gone on like before, thinking I had most of the answers. In actuality, I hadn't even discovered the important questions.

I now close the last of these letters to you, dear Jeff. They have helped me reach out to you during the coma, and in the years of your life after you came out of the coma. They have also helped me come to grips with the realization that the Jeff we once knew was lost to us, and to understand and love the Jeff after the accident. These letters helped me endure our many miles of separation, and to finally face the end of our journey together in this life. And talking to the many people in Texas, whose lives you touched, taught me that your life had great value. You live in my heart and in my thoughts, Jeff. That will not end. And now, Jeff, until we meet again, remember that I love you.

Always,
Mom

P.S. The folks at Kaber were deeply saddened by your passing. How couldn't they be? You were family to them, too. I'm including some letters from the residents and staff, as well as some photos of our family, so you will remember just how much you were loved.

Appendix A

Letters from Staff and
Residents of Kaber Health Care

Letter 1

I read six or seven of Kinky Friedman's mystery novels to Jeff over the years. In each, Kinky would tell his problems to the cat. The recurring line in all of the novels was, "And the cat said . . . nothing." After the first one or two books, whenever I came to that line, I'd halt at the end of the "cat said" phrase, and Jeff would finish the sentence. It is a fond memory I have between us.

He had a strange influence over me when it came to yawning. If I happened to see him yawn, I would yawn, too, even if I tried not to. Eventually, he would yawn just to play with me. I often wondered aloud why he had that effect on me. He'd always say, "Weak mind." Possibly, possibly.

One night, we went to the comedy club with other residents, and Jeff chose to heckle the headliner, who eventually gave him his chance to shine. Jeff told an adult knock-knock joke and was warmly received with laughter and applause. Jeff stood up, took two bows, sat back down, and was happy the rest of the evening.

I miss him.

Letter 2

Oh, Jeffers! I miss the hugs, the laughs, the inappropriate attempts just to get a reaction and keep me on my toes. I'll never forget that 4:14 a.m. "comes real early." :)

It was a blessing working with you, an honor meeting part of your family, and a great pleasure simply knowing you!

You will always be remembered!

Letter 3

Today is September 5, Jeff Westberg. Happy 42nd birthday! I miss you being here. The Kaber community is here to gather to celebrate your life. We always have you in our thoughts.

Letter 4

"Aw, Jeff. You're only as old as you feel."

"Well, hell, I feel 16. Wanna feel?"

Deep sigh! :)

Jeff said so much without saying a word. He made you love him more and more every day. He'd smile and your heart would glow. He'd laugh and you'd laugh along. He called you a "birch," and you knew he cared. To many he was Jeff. To me he was just "Bub."

Thanks for always keeping it real!!

Letter 5

I'll never forget the first time I met Jeff at Kaber. He announced he would show me his "double backflip." I immediately wondered how he would do this in a wheelchair. The staff stepped back to give him room. One staff member even said, "Jeff, you should wear your helmet!" I was beginning to worry about what he was about to do—and that the staff would allow it. How could this be safe?

Jeff rocked in his wheelchair and turned his back to me. He acted like he was about to push back forcefully in his chair. Then he shouted, "Here I go!" I watched as he put both hands behind his head and pointed at me with his middle fingers protruding and laughed and said, "That's my double backflip!"

I will never forget it.

Letter 6

My fondest memory of time spent with Jeff was at Brain Injury Camp two years ago. We had a dance at the end, and Jeff stood up and danced with us. I have never seen him look so happy and carefree. Jeff always made me smile, and now I have a smile on my face whenever I think of him.

Letter 7

I will always remember Jeff with joy and a smile. Every time I saw him, he made my day brighter.

Letter 8

Thanks for the opportunity to care for Jeff. He will be missed greatly. Jeff touched all of the staff and residents who met him. We wish his family the best and know that he will forever be in our hearts and minds.

Letter 9

Never in my life have I met anyone with the charm, jokes, laughter, and humor—as well as the ability to make you love him so much, whether you were pleased with him or disappointed with his actions. Jeff, you taught me to cherish every moment and to not be afraid to laugh at myself. You are forever in my thoughts.

P.S. The Michael Jackson jokes were funnier than I let on, and I use them often! Thanks!

Letter 10

J.D. never met a stranger. He was always kind and considerate to everyone he met. If the world was full of J.D.'s, it would be a much, much nicer place. He will always be sorely missed by everyone who knew him.

Miss you much, Jeff.

Letter 11

What can I say about Jeff that hasn't already been said? Since Jeff left us, we haven't been the same. I'll always remember having a good time hanging out with Jeff. I always will wish I had half the wit he did. Jeff taught me an important lesson. No matter what life hands you, you can still enjoy life. He'll always hold a place in my heart and will never be forgotten.

How could I? He was Jeff.

Letter 12

Thank you for allowing us to share your life. We always had so much fun typing your book on your computer. It has been a blessing to know you and be a part of your story.

Wishing you blue skies and sunshine.

Letter 13

I loved Jeff's double backflips. He was amazingly agile for a man in a wheelchair. I don't remember jokes very well, but I remember the knock-knock joke I heard he told, after a heckler comedian allowed him to take over the stage. And I'll always remember the thickened Dr. Pepper not dripping off me!

Letter 14

He will be missed. He was like everybody's kid brother. Mischief was his middle name. Many of us traveled with him. We all took care of him. He was a hugger, sometimes a real hugger. He had a good sense of humor. He had a good soul. We cared. He knew that.

He will be missed.

Letter 15

One day, Joel and a few others were talking about music, and the subject of Neil Diamond came up. Joel said something Jeff did not like concerning Neil, and Jeff responded to Joel with a resounding expletive.

Jeff always made me laugh. He always had a smart comment or something witty to say. One day, Jeff and I played the piano. Up until that day, I had no idea he could play at all. We had a good time playing both parts to "Heart & Soul." He also played a couple other little pieces his sister had taught him.

I miss Jeff greatly.

Appendix B

Family Photos

Jeff in Boise, age three. He loved to put on funny outfits.

Larry and Carmen, 1967.

Jeff and Carmen at the farmhouse, circa 1969.

Jeff pointing out an "owie" to Amy and Pam, circa 1976.

Pam and Amy posing by the birthday cake, circa 1975. I used to make theme cakes for the kids on their birthdays.

*My mother (Jean) and me, on our last cruise before she died.
Photo taken in Tahiti, 1995.*

*Our Craftsman-style home in Moscow. The window just above the
porch, on the right, was my bedroom. This home stayed in our family
until 1986. My friend Pat O'Hara-Langdon is the artist who painted this
watercolor of our beloved home.*

My mom and dad (Bill and Jean), Chicago, 1943.

My grandma and grandpa (Helen and Conrad)—and me—at the farm, 1949.

Helen and Conrad, wedding photo, February 3, 1920.

Carmen and Larry, wedding photo, October 19, 1968.

Jeff and Carmen. Obviously, I was wanting Calgon to "take me away!"

Pam, Jeff, Jennifer (cousin), and Amy, in the yard at our home in Boise.

Larry and Carmen at Lake Pend Oreille, Idaho, circa 1985.

Family reunion at the farm: Amy, Carey (cousin), Jeff, Justin (cousin),
Jennifer (cousin), and Pam, 4th of July, 1979.

Birthday celebration for my Aunt Helen and Jeff, circa 1982, with friends and relatives.

Carmen, Pam, Amy, Larry and Jeff, circa 1985.

Family gathering at farm. Brother Bill bravely loads Jeff onto a motorcycle for a ride. Various cousins and Amy and Pam running alongside. Summer of 1983.

Celebration of Bill and Jean's 40th wedding anniversary in the summer of 1983. The photo was taken in the yard of their home in Moscow. Left to right: Jennifer, Carey, Amy, Jeff, Cris, Pam, and Justin.

Jeff and Carmen. Jeff is home again and working on exercises.

*In the spa with the family. Jean (my mom), my cousin Kathy,
Aunt Viola, little Kristina, Pam, me, Jeff, and Aunt Helen.*

*Grandma and Grandpa's farmhouse, where we spent our 4th of Julys,
Christmas afternoons, and any weekends I could wheedle as a child.*

Carmen, Jeff, and Amy. This was Amy's last trip to Austin before Jeff died.
Photo taken in the winter of 2007.

Jeff and Amy in Austin, the winter before he died.

Jeff, Amy, Pam, and Sarah (cousin) in Boise.

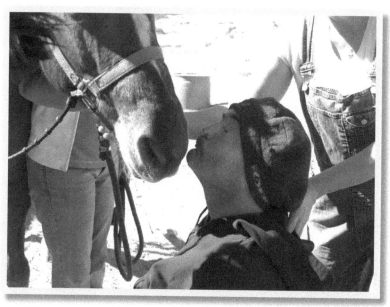

Jeff at the equestrian center in Boise with Pam (behind horse) and a friend.

Family photo on Disney Alaska cruise in July 2018. Larry and I were celebrating our 50th wedding anniversary. Left to right: Lilah, Pam, Carmen, Larry, Amy, Emily, Mr. Taylor, Mrs. Taylor (their first names are both Taylor), and Star.

About the Author

Carmen Westberg grew up in Moscow, Idaho, where she lived until she moved to Boise with her husband Larry in 1968. Carmen earned an accounting degree from Boise State University and worked for the state of Idaho as an auditor and an agency bureau chief until 1999. She and her husband currently spend their time between their homes in Boise and Tucson, where they enjoy golfing, hiking, spending time with family, and socializing with their friends.

Dear Jeff is Carmen's first book.

CPSIA information can be obtained
at www.ICGtesting.com
Printed in the USA
FSHW010606150419
57259FS